Teaching with Technology

CHANDOS
INFORMATION PROFESSIONAL SERIES

Series Editor: Ruth Rikowski
(email: Rikowskigr@aol.com)

Chandos' new series of books are aimed at the busy information professional. They have been specially commissioned to provide the reader with an authoritative view of current thinking. They are designed to provide easy-to-read and (most importantly) practical coverage of topics that are of-interest to librarians and other information professionals. If you would like a full listing of current and forthcoming titles, please visit our web site **www.chandospublishing.com** or contact Hannah Grace-Williams on email info@chandospublishing.com or telephone number +44 (0) 1865 884447.

New authors: we are always pleased to receive ideas for new titles; if you would like to write a book for Chandos, please contact Dr Glyn Jones on email gjones@chandospublishing.com or telephone number +44 (0) 1865 884447.

Bulk orders: some organisations buy a number of copies of our books. If you are interested in doing this, we would be pleased to discuss a discount. Please contact Hannah Grace-Williams on email info@chandospublishing.com or telephone number +44 (0) 1865 884447.

Teaching with Technology: An academic librarian's guide

EDITED BY
JOE M. WILLIAMS
AND
SUSAN P. GOODWIN

Chandos Publishing
Oxford · England

Chandos Publishing (Oxford) Limited
Chandos House
5 & 6 Steadys Lane
Stanton Harcourt
Oxford OX29 5RL
UK
Tel: +44 (0) 1865 884447 Fax: +44 (0) 1865 884448
Email: info@chandospublishing.com
www.chandospublishing.com

First published in Great Britain in 2007

ISBN:
978 1 84334 172 7 (paperback)
978 1 84334 173 4 (hardback)
1 84334 172 7 (paperback)
1 84334 173 5 (hardback)

© The contributors, 2007

Typeset by Domex e-Data Pvt. Ltd.
Printed in the UK and USA.

Contents

List of figures and tables

Figures

Tables

About the contributors

B. Lynn Eades, MLS, AHIP, is web development librarian in the Application Development Services Department at the Health Sciences Library, University of North Carolina at Chapel Hill. She has a BSc in telecommunications from Ball State University and an MLS from Indiana University. Her responsibilities include maintaining and improving the Health Sciences Library's website and investigating new internet technologies and their potential use in the library. She has been teaching the use of the internet for the past 14 years, and currently teaches a class on using RSS as a research tool.

Susan Fliss, MA, MLS, is the director of education and outreach for the Dartmouth College Library. Education & Outreach, the library's education programme, fosters collaboration in teaching and learning among faculty, students, staff and librarians to advance information literacy. Susan's interests include professional development of librarians as teachers, use of instructional technology in information literacy education and library initiatives with other campus partners such as teaching centres, writing programmes and curricular computing.

Susan P. Goodwin is associate professor and coordinator of instructional services at Texas A&M University Libraries. For the past five years she has developed and delivered instruction and information literacy initiatives for Texas

A&M University Libraries, having worked previously as a course developer for Athabasca University, Canada.

Barrie E. Hayes, MSLS, is head of application development services at the Health Sciences Library, University of North Carolina at Chapel Hill. She has a BSc in biology from North Carolina State University and an MSc in library sciences from the UNC School of Information and Library Science. Her background is in reference and systems development, serving as manager of the Health Sciences Library's UNCLE Digital Library for eight years. In addition to leading the Application Development Services Department in support of the library's digital priorities, Barrie's professional interests include information architecture, project management, digital libraries and technologies that support collaborative research and knowledge-sharing in the biomedical sciences. She is a wiki user and is currently investigating wiki systems to support collaborative writing and content management activities in the Health Sciences Library.

Barbara Knauff, PhD, is a senior instructional technologist in curricular computing at Dartmouth College. In this role she supports Blackboard, Dartmouth's course management system. She also teaches workshops and works with faculty on other technologies that facilitate teaching and learning, such as custom course websites, blogs, wikis and multimedia projects. Her interest in pedagogy and learning outcomes goes back to her previous career as a college French professor.

Megan Oakleaf, MLS, PhD, is an assistant professor in the School of Information Studies, Syracuse University, Syracuse, NY. She is a former public school teacher and academic instruction librarian and currently teaches graduate reference and library assessment courses. She has previously published and presented on online instructional techniques and assessment of student learning outcomes.

Jane Quigley, MSLS, is head of Kresge Physical Sciences Library at Dartmouth College and has worked closely with the library's Education & Outreach programme since its inception in 2002. Jane is involved in integrating librarian participation and library resources into the Blackboard CMS.

Jennifer Sharkey is assistant professor of library science and the information integration librarian at the Purdue University Libraries. She received her MA in library and information science from the University of Wisconsin-Madison and an MS in higher education administration from Mankato State University. Jennifer partners with faculty across campus, helping them incorporate information literacy into their curricula and enhance their course projects with multimedia components. Her research interests include creative integration of information literacy and technology into curricula as well as the application of graphic design, instructional design and web design principles to teaching initiatives. Currently she is a member of the ACRL Instruction Section's instructional technologies committee. Her recent publications include 'Towards information fluency: applying a different model to an information literacy credit course' in *Reference Services Review* and a chapter on 'Integrating technology literacy and information literacy' in the book *Technology Literacy Uses in Learning Environments.*

Amy VanScoy, MA, MLS, is assistant head of research and information services at NCSU Libraries, North Carolina State University, Raleigh, NC. She co-manages virtual reference services at NCSU Libraries and trains librarians to provide the service. She has previously published on other virtual reference issues, including privacy in virtual reference and remote reference to patrons within the library.

Colleen Wheeler is the assistant director for web strategy at Wheaton College in Norton, Massachusetts. She serves on the board of trustees for the North East Regional Computing Program (NERCOMP) and on the advisory board for the Susan Vogt Leadership Fellows Program. She has written and presented extensively about learning and collaboration. A teacher and trombonist, she has developed several technology-enabled music education programmes including performances, coaching sessions and lectures conducted over Internet2.

Calvin Williams, MLS, is the associate vice president of instructional technology at Monmouth University, providing managerial leadership and planning for the delivery of instructional technology services in support of faculty, students and academic staff. Prior to joining Monmouth in 2005, Calvin was director of the Teaching, Learning and Technology Center at Seton Hall University, responsible for management of the instructional design staff who assist faculty with teaching and learning initiatives and the incorporation of technology. His previous career includes posts at the University of Wisconsin's (Madison) Division of Information Technology and the Center for Teaching, Learning, & Technology at Bowling Green State University in Ohio. He is a graduate of Rutgers University.

Joe M. Williams is director of the learning commons at North Carolina State University Libraries. He has several years' experience integrating technologies with library services and delivering library instruction over the web. In the past five years he has spoken at conferences across the country, mainly on the implementation and use of new technologies in teaching and learning.

List of acronyms

AAC	Advanced Audio Coding
ACLU	American Civil Liberties Union
ACRL	Association of College and Research Libraries
AVI	Audio Video Interleave
CALEA	Communications Assistance for Law Enforcement Act
CI2	Composers of Internet2
CMS	course management system
CNI	Coalition for Networked Information
COPPUL	Council of Prairie and Pacific University Libraries
eTIPS	Educational Technology Integration and Implementation Principles
FAS	Federation of American Scientists
IEEE	Institute of Electrical and Electronics Engineers
ILS	integrated library systems
IP	Internet Protocol
LMS	learning management system
NERCOMP	North East Regional Computing Program
NITLE	National Institute for Technology in Liberal Education
NSF	National Science Foundation
OCLC	Online Computer Library Center

OSHEAN	Ocean State Higher Education Economic Development and Administrative Network
PDA	personal digital assistant
RDF	resource document framework
RINET	Rhode Island Network for Educational Technology
RSS	RDF site summary
RSS	real simple syndication
RSS	rich site summary
TILT	Texas Information Literacy Tutorial
VLE	virtual learning environment
VOD	video on demand
VoIP	voice over IP
VPN	virtual private network
WEP	Wired Equivalancy Protocol
WLAN	wireless local area network
WPAN	wireless personal area network

Introduction
Joe M. Williams

Instruction and technology both play integral roles in librarianship today. There are many books addressing teaching within the library, and many more that provide librarians with an overview of current technologies. This handbook strives to bring these two relevant topics together in a practical overview of instructional uses and applications of today's popular technologies. The book is not designed to be read cover to cover, but referred to over time as the reader considers incorporating a particular technology in instruction (such as establishing an instruction blog), or perhaps begins reflecting on current uses of a familiar product or service (such as chat-based reference). Initially you may wish to browse through the entire handbook, in order to gain a sense of the breadth and depth of topics covered.

Many of the technologies discussed here are beginning to bleed together, making it challenging at times to separate some topics completely by chapter, such as podcasting and screencasting. Each chapter of this handbook addresses one or a group of similar technologies by providing basic background technical information, some examples of potential instructional applications, contemplation on the future directions of each technology and a list of references and suggested reading. All the chapter authors are academic librarians or instructional technologists with first-hand experience using and evaluating a particular application or service. Within the book's basic structure, the individual authors have approached their topics differently as they saw fit.

Chapter 1 examines screencasting, from creating and captioning video files to adding quizzes and summarising some current screencasting software options. Chapter 2 addresses other related forms of online publication – podcasting, blogs, wikis and RSS – outlining the differences and similarities of each and providing examples of their instructional uses and potential. Chapter 3 looks at virtual reference and instruction tools and services from both technical and pedagogical points of view. The fourth chapter discusses various aspects of mobile computing, which leads into a related discussion of learning spaces – increasingly mobile and personalised environments – in Chapter 5. Chapter 6 reviews course management systems such as Blackboard. These online course environments often incorporate many of the technologies mentioned in previous chapters, such as chat-based communication and screencasting. The last chapter discusses videoconferencing, offering a clear overview of exciting voice-over-internet-protocol advancements as well as several engaging, real-life examples of the technology in use.

As librarians know so well, current technologies and library services are both changing at a rapid pace. It is often difficult to select appropriate technologies to meet a library's instructional needs, learn the basics of those selected applications and then research useful library applications before the technologies become outdated or overshadowed by the 'next big thing'. We hope this handbook provides a quick and useful overview of some of today's most current technologies, and that it helps you choose those technologies that will enhance and define your changing instructional services.

Screencasting 101: online video tutorials for library instruction

Susan P. Goodwin

Creation of online videos for library instruction is not new, but the technology that allows us to create these videos has greatly improved over the last few years. Software rich with editing features, smaller learning curves and multiple file format options have made it much easier and less time-consuming to produce quality tutorials. As a result, this medium is becoming an increasingly popular choice for the design and delivery of library instruction in an online environment.

This chapter will focus on one particular niche within the online tutorial movement, that of screencasting. The term 'screencast' was first coined by Jon Udell (2004). A screencast is a digital recording of actions that take place on a computer screen, often accompanied by step-by-step audio narration (Udell, 2005). While a screenshot provides a static visual of what appears on a user's monitor for a particular moment in time, a screencast puts the screen in motion for a particular period of time to show all screen activity, including mouse clicks and keyboard strokes plus any accompanying sounds.

In the early to mid-1990s early adopters of screencasting used software products like Lotus ScreenCam to produce basic instructional videos on how to search online databases (Peek and Powers, 1995; Jackson, 1999). The software, still in its infancy, was rudimentary and had very limited editing capabilities. File sizes also tended to be quite large, which posed problems for both hosting and viewing the videos.

In the last five years new software products have emerged, bringing screencasting to the masses and more prominently into the world of library instruction. Screencasting allows librarians to create self-paced video tutorials that demonstrate particular online resources and services the library has to offer, as well as specific websites and other software applications.

Anatomy of a screencast

There are three basic steps involved in creating a screencast. The first is to record the video (Figure 1.1). Before recording can begin one must determine how much of the computer screen to capture. Most programs offer the ability to capture the full screen or a particular region of the screen. To reduce the overall file size of the screencast it is best to record only as much of the screen as is needed. Udell (2005) suggests cropping the video as much as possible so your viewers can focus in on the important action on the screen.

If you plan to add narration to a screencast a microphone is required. Most software products allow you to do a sound check before proceeding with the recording. This helps to ensure sound levels are set correctly for optimal playback. Recording tools work much like the features on DVD or VCR players. Simply click the record button to begin and

Figure 1.1 Example of recorder tool (Camtasia Studio 4)

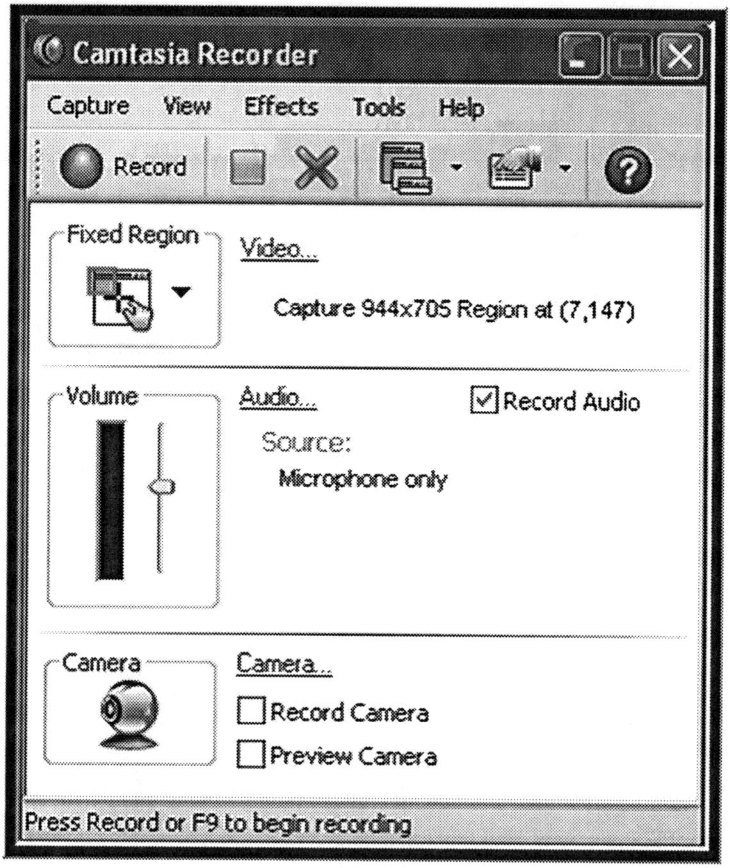

use the stop or pause buttons to halt recording once you have completed your on-screen demonstration.

The Camtasia Studio software from TechSmith (Figure 1.1) is an example of a screencasting product that records full motion video. Other products like Qarbon's ViewletBuilder capture a series of still screens that are then joined together via animation in the editing stage of production.

Once an initial recording has been made the file is ready to be edited. In this stage the raw video file, or individual screen captures, can be viewed and manipulated on a storyboard. Mistakes made during the initial recording can be cut out of the file and additional pieces can be spliced in to replace them. Voice narration, if not already recorded in the original file, can often be added to the video during this phase of the production process. Some software products allow for additional layers of sound, making the inclusion of background music possible.

In addition to basic correctional edits further instructional enhancements can be made to the file during the editing stage. Most software packages include the ability to add callouts (Figure 1.2), title screens, mouse and cursor special effects, text and screen highlighting for added emphasis and much more.

Hotspots for textual input and quizzes (Figure 1.3) can be added to engage the viewer in specific activities on screen as he or she moves through a tutorial, making the screencasts more interactive.

Once editing is complete files are ready to be saved. Most software products provide a list of output options from which to choose (Figure 1.4). Converting the raw video files is simple thanks to built-in wizards that walk you through the process. The software section of this chapter will provide more detailed information about the types of file options available for completed screencasts.

While screencasts can be saved as individual files, most software products also provide various options for organising and presenting collections of thematic videos. Very little time needs to be spent developing attractive webpages to house your instructional videos: one can use the software to create visually appealing CD and DVD menus, webpage menus and more.

From quick-and-dirty demonstrations to full production tutorials complete with interactive screens and online

Figure 1.2 Example of callout feature (Camtasia Studio 4)

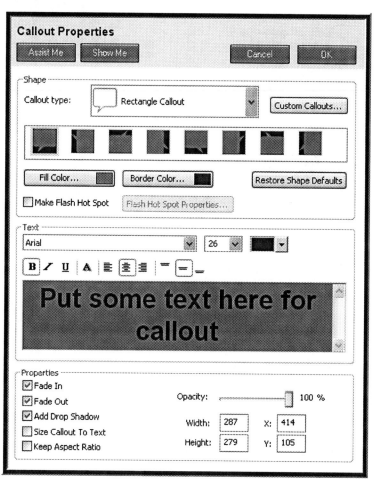

quizzes, screencasts can be as simple or as complex as you want them to be. Classroom database instruction can be supplemented with more in-depth search examples via screencasts; FAQ lists of screencasts can be developed to assist reference staff in answering complex database search questions at the reference desk or in a virtual reference environment; even entire classroom instruction sessions can

Figure 1.3 Example of quiz tool (Camtasia Studio 4)

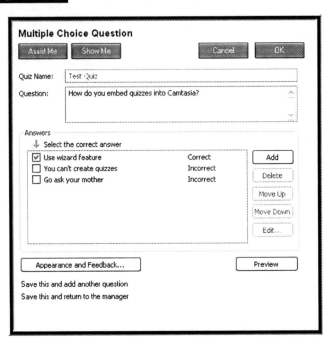

be recorded live and then made available on the web for students to review after class or in place of class.

Other possible library applications for screencasts include:

- demonstrations of online searching techniques for specific library databases;

- promotional videos demonstrating new (or not so new) online services or resources (e.g. a virtual reference service or online renewal of library books);

- demonstrations of how to use specific desktop applications such as citation software;

- current awareness videos featuring new web resources and tools (e.g. a demonstration on how to use iTunes to download music to an iPod);

Figure 1.4 Example of output file options (Camtasia Studio 4)

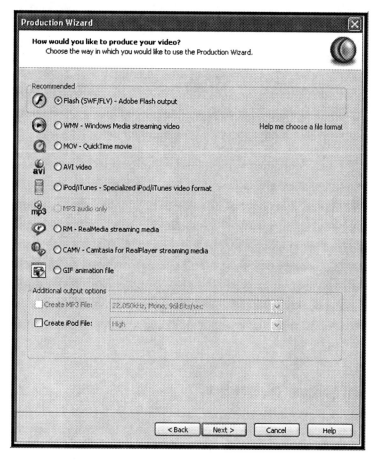

- virtual tours of websites or actual libraries using screen recordings and traditional video;

- video essays on how to evaluate information resources on the web;

- interviews with library staff or (even better) students or faculty members demonstrating how they use a particular library service or resource and why they find it useful for their research;

- unedited recordings of staff training sessions can be made available on the library's intranet for review and content from the staff training sessions can be edited to create more professional training videos quickly for the public;

- comprehensive instruction packages on DVD or the web for distance education students containing targeted tutorials demonstrating relevant online services and resources to support their coursework at a distance.

If you do not have the time or inclination to create your own screencasts you can still incorporate them into your instruction programme by linking to tutorials already available on the web. Many database vendors now make screencasts available on their help pages. You can also take part in cooperative screencasting projects with other institutions to save yourself valuable time. Specific examples of screencasts used in library instruction and beyond are provided in the 'Additional resources' section of this chapter.

Software overview

There are a number of screencasting software packages available for purchase, as well as a few free programs available on the web. All provide the basic tools needed to get you started. Creating screencasts has not only become a relatively easy task but much more fun given the number of new editing and production features that continue to appear as new versions of these software products are released.

Early screencasters faced basic technology challenges, such as the ever-increasing need for server storage space for large video files and end-user issues such as media player compatibility problems and insufficient bandwidth. In many cases viewers with dial-up connections could not watch the tutorials. Further, patrons without the proper media player already installed were required to upgrade to a new version or download a totally different media player in order to view the videos (Xiao et al., 2004: 372–3).

The development of Flash format files in the early 1990s completely revolutionised screencasts by making them exceptionally user-friendly. Unlike other media players such as Windows Media Player, Quicktime and RealPlayer, the Flash Player comes pre-installed on 98 per cent of all desktop computers (Adobe, 2006). This has eliminated the need for screencasters to make videos available in multiple file formats (although it is now easier than ever to do so).

End-user access issues also saw improvements throughout the 1990s. Broadband became more accessible to the public and advancements in file compression techniques made viewing screencasts for the average library patron easier, and in some cases now possible. That said, completed screencasts can still be quite large in size. Notess (2005: 45) estimates each minute of video corresponds to roughly one megabyte in file size.

A nice addition to some of the current screencasting products is the ability to export the content into print-friendly formats such as Microsoft Word, PDF and plain text documents, thereby eliminating the need to produce accompanying handouts and supportive documentation manually. The ability to provide printed documentation alongside multimedia files helps to address multiple learning styles inside and outside the classroom.

Developers have also given consideration to new web technologies and multimedia devices. With the rise in popularity of portable media devices such as iPods, multimedia websites such as iTunes and YouTube and web applications such as blogs, podcasts and RSS feeds, look for new output options such as MP3 files, iTunes-compatible files and automatically generated RSS feeds. These features are already available with some screencasting software products.

Another relatively new feature is the ability to add closed captioning to video files. Now full transcripts can be displayed on screen to help support the hearing impaired. Transcripts can also be translated into various languages to support diverse audiences. If you have a large international student population this is an easy way to make your videos more accessible with minimal effort. Closed captioning is also a valuable feature for use in computer labs and library settings where speakers and headphones are often not available to the public.

To support self-paced learning better, new and improved presentation options allow videos to be easily broken down into well-organised segments. Some software products offer built-in branching features that allow you to create multiple learning pathways. This feature is great for scenario-based learning and for empowering end-users to decide how they want to progress through a tutorial. Branching is the perfect way to demonstrate the multiple ways in which a search can be conducted in any one database. Completed tutorials offer the patron a choice of flexible learning pathways. If a user is more interested in how to develop a detailed search using a variety of search limits he or she can move through an increasingly complex set of searches that demonstrate some of the database's more powerful features. If a patron is more interested in how to save, organise and e-mail search results he or she can quickly move from a basic search to a series of detailed videos on how to save and manipulate citations found within the database.

Interactive tutorials were not possible in the early days of screencasting. With the birth of Flash in the mid-1990s many libraries opted to create more interactive multimedia tutorials rather than focus on screencasts. Flash tutorials in comparison to basic screencasting tutorials took much more time and technical expertise. TILT (Texas Information Literacy Tutorial), the gold standard of information literacy tutorials, was developed using a host of Macromedia software products including Dreamweaver, Director and Flash. Production began in 1997, with the first tutorials coming online in 1999 (University of Texas System Digital Library, 2004). While highly engaging and professionally produced, this project took several years to develop and required the technical expertise of a number of developers and knowledge of instructional design techniques.

While TILT and other tutorials that emulate it are still a popular choice for online instruction, screencasting has gained ground with the addition of some new interactive software features. Built-in quizzes and surveys using multiple choice, true/false and open-ended questions are now easy to generate thanks to simple user interfaces and wizards. Additional interactive features such as text entry areas, click zones and hotspots further engage end-users by prompting them to perform certain skill-testing tasks at various points throughout a screencast. In addition to viewing (and listening to) rich on-screen demonstrations, screencasters can now inject learning simulations into their movies to get their audience actively involved.

These advancements in technology, especially the new interactive components of screencasting, will no doubt help to increase the popularity of this genre as a tool for library instruction. The list below provides a sampling of software products currently available.

CamStudio

Available at: www.camstudio.org.
Platform: Windows.
Cost: free.

- Free streaming video software.

- Record all screen activity along with voice narration.

- Completed files are in AVI format but can then be converted to streaming Flash videos using the accompanying SWF producer.

- No built-in video editing capabilities.

- Good for short and simple recordings that do not require editing.

Camtasia Studio (TechSmith)

Available at: www.techsmith.com/camtasia.asp.
Platform: Windows.
Cost: $179 (educational price) or $199 bundled with SnagIt Studio.

- Free 30-day trial available.

- Comprehensive recording, editing and production package.

- Add audio during or after screen recording or record voice-only files in MP3 format to publish on the web as podcasts.

- Picture-in-picture format allows for a talking-head video to be played in tandem with screen recordings, or one can easily produce mixed video files with both talking-head video and screen recordings.

- New editing tool helps to edit out unwanted background noise from files.

- Record and publish PowerPoint files within PowerPoint using the Camtasia Studio toolbar.

- Supports closed captioning, clickable hotspots and callouts and interactive quizzes and surveys (allows instructional feedback during quiz, as well as open-ended questions in addition to multiple choice and true/false).

■ Numerous features available for adding emphasis to recorded videos, including zoom and pan tools, customised callout features, cursor effects, text and screen highlighting and more.

■ Export finished products to MP3, iPod Video, Flash (SWF, FLV), AVI, WMV, QuickTime (MOV), RealMedia (RM), animated GIF, EXE files and more.

■ Supports creation of clickable table of contents for a single video or to link together multiple videos.

■ Additional SnagIt tool good for creating and manipulating basic screenshots and includes ability to add narration.

Captivate (Adobe/Macromedia)

Available at: www.adobe.com/products/captivate/.
Platform: Windows.
Cost: $199 (educational price).

■ Free 30-day trial available.

■ Comprehensive recording, editing and production package.

■ Full motion recording of screen actions.

■ Add audio during or after initial recording.

■ Comprehensive quiz options allow for instructional feedback and ability to capture scoring data from quizzes (including text entry).

■ Actively supports scenario-based learning with new branching feature that allows for end-user customised learning paths.

■ Integrate talking-head video into captured slides using transparencies.

- Supports closed captioning.

- Numerous special effect features available, including zoom, customised captions, text and screen area highlights and greyouts, PowerPoint import options.

- Easily integrated with other Macromedia products such as Breeze, Flash, Authorware etc., and anticipate further integration with specific Adobe tools and programs.

- Export finished products to Flash (SWF), TXT, Word (DOC), PDF, e-mail, Pocket PC files and more.

- Supports automatic generation of a variety of handouts (storyboards, step-by-step documentation, lesson plans and more).

TurboDemo (Bernard D&G)

Available at: www.turbodemo.com/eng/index.htm.
Platform: Windows, Mac, UNIX, Linux.
Cost: professional version single-user licence $629 (educational pricing available).

- Free 30-day trial available.

- Comprehensive recording, editing and production package.

- Supports a variety of platforms, unlike its competitors.

- Screenshots captured one by one with click of the mouse; slides are then joined together to create a single video file.

- Slides can be edited to include callouts, audio and interactive hotspots for learning simulation.

- Supports interactive quizzing.

- Export finished products to Flash (SWF), WMV, TXT, Java applets, GIF animated, Word (DOC), PDF, Windows ASF and AVI, EXE files and more.

14

ViewletBuilder (Qarbon)

Available at: www.qarbon.com/presentation-software /viewletbuilder/.
Platform: Windows, Linux.

- Screenshots are captured one by one as defined by the user, then slides are joined together using the ViewletBuilder tool to create a single video file.

- Each screenshot slide can be edited to include callouts, audio and clickable hotspots for learning simulation, hyperlinks, notes and interactive quizzes.

- Supports scenario-based learning with branching and hyperlinking options allowing for end-user customisation.

- Numerous special effect features available, including interactive click and text zones, customised captions, callouts and cursors, text and screen area highlighting.

- Supports interactive quizzing.

- Full motion video capture and PowerPoint capture/record capabilities available via Qarbon's ViewletCam software ($119 educational pricing or $279 educational price for Builder/Cam bundle).

- Export finished products to Flash (SWF) and EXE, and slides as image files to PDF, JPEG, GIF, PNG, TIFF, BMP and more.

Wink

Available at: www.debugmode.com/wink.
Platform: Windows, Linux.
Cost: free.

- Freeware program for capturing screenshots and adding voice narration.

- Editing options are rudimentary but include ability to create basic text boxes, callouts and shapes, as well as navigational buttons.
- Completed files can be exported to PDF, HTML, SWF (Flash) and EXE formats.

What will we think of next?

In October 2005 the Federation of American Scientists (FAS) brought together leading representatives from the entertainment software industry with members of the National Science Foundation to explore and assess how modern video and computer games are now providing 'a rich landscape of adventure and challenge that appeal to a growing number of Americans' (FAS, 2006: 3). Cited directly from the report, some of the major areas explored included:

- what aspects of learning are most amenable to new approaches offered by games?
- what kinds of research are needed to identify features of gaming?
- what can be effective in education and training?
- what kinds of changes in instructional practices and management of educational institutions are needed to take advantage of the power games could bring to teaching and learning? (FAS, 2006: 4)

As the report concludes, 'there was a strong consensus among the summit participants that there are many features of digital games, including game design approaches and digital game technologies, which can be applied to address the increasing demand for high quality education' (FAS, 2006: 4).

Further, a recent study by the Pew Internet & American Life Project on the gaming habits of college students found that over 70 per cent of students reported playing games 'at least once in a while'. Around two-thirds (65 per cent) reported being 'regular' or 'occasional' gamers (Jones, 2003: 2).

Does the gaming phenomenon have anything to tell those of us who are interested in the intersection of screencasting technology and educational initiatives? Traditionalists (cynics?) will no doubt chafe at the thought. Others, perhaps more open to the social and technological trends unfolding around us, may see within the rise of gaming a nascent opportunity.

Readers who are interested in exploring new directions for screencasting technology in instructional environments may wish to consider this emerging area. Why? Simply because gaming designs can, and the author predicts will soon, be incorporated into screencasts using the new interactive features built into the software.

Additional resources

Sample screencasts

- *ANTS: Animated Tutorial Sharing Project* (www. brandonu.ca/Library/COPPUL/index.html).
  Cooperative tutorial project begun by COPPUL librarians (Council of Prairie and Pacific University Libraries – a consortium of 20 university libraries located in Manitoba, Saskatchewan, Alberta and British Columbia). The goal is to create a comprehensive resource of online tutorials available for public use. Librarians from outside COPPUL can participate in the venture by simply signing on to produce and/or update tutorials for any of the

needed online resources listed in the COPPUL tutorials wiki (http://wiki.uwinnipeg.ca/index.php/COPPUL_ Tutorials).

- *Critical Thinking and Screencasts* (www.adcritic.com/ interactive/view.php?id=5927).
  This screencast from the ACLU explores the issues of identity and privacy. It is an example of how screencasts can be used to present material that is more 'what if' than 'how to'.

- *Central Michigan University Off-Campus Library Services* (http://ocls.cmich.edu/help/overview/index.html).
  Good example of how individual screencasts and talking-head video can be packaged and presented on the web in a well-organised and visually appealing way. Captivate videos.

- *David Lee King testing CamStudio* (www.davidleeking .com/2006/12/11/library-catalog-usability-and-a-test-of-camstudio/).
  King takes a test drive of CamStudio for a quick usability review of a library catalogue.

- *Class guide screencasts for distance education students* (http://library.tamu.edu/portal/site/Library/menuitem.95e 060d328c5ba7869e19cf419008a0c/?vgnextoid=a8eec9b 4b2bdb010VgnVCM1000007800a8c0RCRD).
  Various screencasts embedded into a class guide for distance education students.

- *Librarycasting SE: screencasts, podcasts, tutorials and titles for the sciences and engineering* (http://blog.vcu .edu/lse/screencasts_all_videos).
  Subject-specific blog from Virginia Commonwealth University Libraries that promotes various multimedia instructional resources for the sciences and engineering. Includes links to library-made screencasts and promotes other useful screencasts available for free on the web.

- *University of Calgary Library screencasts* (http://library .ucalgary.ca/services/libraryconnection/tutorials.php). Provides a good sampling of instructional screencasts using different software packages (Camtasia, Captivate and Qarbon videos).

Software support

- *7 Things You Should Know About Screencasting* (www.educause.edu/content.asp?page_id=666&ID=ELI7 012&bhcp=1). From the EDUCAUSE Resource Center, this handout provides a good summary of screencasting technology.

- *30 Demos in 30 Days* (http://video.techsmith.com/ blog/screencasts/tss/dv/30d30d/30_Demos_in_30_Days .html). Helpful screencasts from TechSmith demonstrating how to use particular features of their Camtasia Studio software.

- *Libcasting: screencasting and libraries* (http://notess.com/ screencasting/). New blog by Greg Notess (reference librarian at Montana State University). Explores all things screencasting from the perspective of a librarian. Entries so far include links to relevant workshops, software comparisons and critiques and general advice on how to create screencasts.

- *Library success: a best practices wiki* (www.libsuccess .org/index.php?title=Online_Tutorials). Contribute to the 'online tutorial' page or check in from time to time to see what is new on this wiki. Read from a growing list of tips on how to develop quality online tutorials. Provides links to exemplary online tutorials as well as useful blogs and websites to watch, plus software recommendations.

For inspiration...

- *Gaming in libraries.*
  Levine (2006) is a guide in this area.

- *Udell screencasts* (http://del.icio.us/judell/screencast+jonudell).
  This website provides a comprehensive listing of Jon Udell's screencasts. Jon's screencasting style is very casual yet informative: one always feels like one is tuning in to an old friend when watching his 'shows'. For example, the 'Heavy metal umlaut' demonstrative screencast shows how pages evolve on Wikipedia (http://weblog.infoworld.com/udell/gems/umlaut.html); 'Documenting the flood' demonstrates how you can mix on-screen video with traditional video to create a documentary-style screencast (http://weblog.infoworld.com/udell/gems/KeeneFlood.html).

- Zefrank (www.zefrank.com).
  If humour awards were given out for screencasts Ze would win hands down. While not academic in nature, his 'educational videos' are fun and might provide some ideas for your own productions. An FAQ list for research help designed after his 'My advice to you' interactive screencast video might be a fun way to engage students (www.zefrank.com/advice/); for an example of side-by-side talking-head video with corresponding screencast see www.zefrank.com/punc/. Follow Ze's blog and resource page to spark some creative ideas of your own. Ze's talking frog usability screencasts (http://frogreview.com) are informative and funny: see how the frogs fare at

buying tickets for U2 on the TicketMaster website
(www.frogreview.com/m/05/11/ticketmaster/).

References

Adobe (2006) 'FAQ', Adobe Systems Incorporated; available
at: *www.adobe.com/products/flashplayer/productinfo/
faq/* (accessed: 31 December 2006).

FAS (2006) 'Harnessing the power of video games for
learning', summit on educational games, 25 October
2005, Washington, DC, Federation of American
Scientists; available at: *www.fas.org/gamesummit/
Resources/Summit%20on%20Educational%20Games
.pdf* (accessed: 31 December 2006).

Jackson, Cathie (1999) 'Computer-based video: a tool for
information skills training?', *Aslib Proceedings*, 51:
213–23.

Jones, Steve (2003) 'Let the games begin: gaming technology
and entertainment among college students', Pew Internet
& American Life Project; available at: *www.pewinternet
.org/pdfs/PIP_College_Gaming_Reporta.pdf* (accessed:
31 December 2006).

Levine, Jenny (2006) 'Gaming and libraries: intersection of
services', Library Technology Reports 42.5. Chicago:
American Library Association.

Notess, Greg R. (2005) 'Casting the net: podcasting and
screencasting', *Online*, 29(6): 43–5.

Peek, Robin and Powers, Allison (1995) 'Doing a computer-
based demonstration? There may be a better way',
Journal of Academic Librarianship, 21(6): 481–3.

Udell, Jon (2004) 'Name that genre: screencast', 17
November; available at: *http://weblog.infoworld.com/
udell/2004/11/17.html* (accessed: 31 December 2006).

Udell, Jon (2005) 'What is screencasting?', 16 November; available at: *http://digitalmedia.oreilly.com/2005/11/16/what-is-screencasting.html* (accessed: 31 December 2006).

University of Texas System Digital Library (2004) 'TILT: project development and acknowledgments'; available at: *http://tilt.lib.utsystem.edu/resources/devt.html* (accessed: 29 December 2006).

Xiao, Daniel Y., Pietraszewski, Barbara A. and Goodwin, Susan P. (2004) 'Full stream ahead: database instruction through online videos', *Library Hi Tech*, 22(4): 366–74.

2

Blogs, wikis, RSS and podcasting: Web 2.0 tools for academic librarians and educators

B. Lynn Eades and Barrie E. Hayes

In 2005 Tim O'Reilly coined the phrase 'Web 2.0'. In his article 'What is Web 2.0?' he identified the applications that define this new web environment (O'Reilly, 2005), including weblogs, wikis and syndication. Libraries are beginning to incorporate these applications as a means to create more interactive, user-centred library services, sometimes referred to as Library 2.0. According to Michael Casey and Laura Savastinuk (2006: 40), 'the heart of Library 2.0 is user-centered change'. Patrons are no longer just people we serve, but potential collaborators. As we engage them using these Web 2.0 applications, we gain new opportunities to understand their information needs, interact with them in new ways and demonstrate the value of library resources and services.

Weblogs

Weblogs (pronounced 'we'-blogs, but usually just shortened to blogs) can take on many forms, including personal journals or diaries, platforms for political views, news outlets and research outlets for information-sharing and collaboration. Blogs are websites that usually have at least three of the following traits: entries appear in a reverse chronological order; entries listed in specific categories that can be searched; links to other sites of interest and places for comments; and a monthly archive of previous entries.

Tim Berners-Lee, the father of the World Wide Web, is credited with having the precursor to the blog. His listings of new websites that had come on to the internet were presented in reverse chronological order and were archived monthly. They were soon abandoned when the web grew at such an exponential rate that keeping the list current was just too great a task (Bausch et al., 2002: 8–9). The late 1990s saw the blog take on another form, personal journals. Sites such as LiveJournal (www.livejournal.com/) gave individuals a place to create their own piece of cyberspace, without having to learn HTML. They could now share their views, images and feelings with hundreds of others on the web and get feedback from these new friends. Yet blogs came to prominence after the tragic events of 11 September 2001. With people clamouring for news and the regular news outlets overwhelmed, many found the personal accounts of those near the tragedy more moving than any news story.

Today blogs are so mainstream that major news magazines like *Time* and *Newsweek* showcase blogs of interest in their pages. Political candidates, such as Howard Dean and John Kerry, have used blogs to get their agendas before the voters. Libraries are also seeing the value of blogs for promoting the library and its services. Anything that can appear on a website can appear within a blog.

Creating your blog

Before you can create a blog, you will need to decide upon a program. Blogs can be hosted online or installed on a local server.

Online hosting offers an easy and quick way to create a blog (Figure 2.1). For librarians with little to no knowledge of HTML, a hosted online blog is the perfect solution. Two of the best-known services are Blogger (www.blogger.com) and WordPress (www.wordpress.com). Both services are free to use.

If a library has some knowledge of HTML or a good IT staff, it may want to download a blogging program and host it locally. There are many open-access programs available for blogs. One of the most used is Moveable Type (www.moveabletype.com).

There are advantages and disadvantages to both these solutions (Table 2.1).

Figure 2.1　Blogger home page

Table 2.1   Online-hosted versus locally installed blogs

	Advantages	Disadvantages
Hosted online	No HTML knowledge needed Can be up and running in a day Updates and maintenance are handled by the host Security is handled by the host	Separate address from your library website Not as flexible on page design Site may disappear or charge for their services in the future
Locally installed	More control over the look and feel More popular solution for multiple blogs	Responsibility for updates and maintenance Responsibility for security and software Requires more technical knowledge Takes more than a day to implement

Whether you use an online service or host it locally, you will need to decide what features your blog should incorporate. The following are some to consider.

- *Archives*. Will the hosting service or locally installed version have an archive? If you are using a hosting service, is there a size limit on your archive? Is the archive created automatically or do you have to archive the material yourself?

- *Categories*. Can you create multiple categories for your blog? Is there a limit?

- *Search*. Is the search feature included or will you have to create this yourself? What information is searched?

- *Community tools*. Can more than one person be allowed to post an entry? Are replies automatically posted or can you preview them before posting? Can the reply feature be turned off?

- *Subscription links.* Will users want to have entries sent to their e-mail through a list service? Can this be set up through the software?

- *Syndication.* Is an RSS feed automatically created? What type of feed is created (RSS or Atom)?

A very useful comparison of blog software features and services is available on the web at www.ojr.org/ojr/images/ blog_software_comparison.cfm.

Teaching with blogs

Blogs provide a fast and easy way to get information out to your audience. Since blog entries can be a few sentences to several paragraphs, no item is too small or too big. Here are just a few ways libraries have used blogs.

- *Replace a standard web subject guide with a blog.* At Georgia State University the subject specialists use blogs instead of the old web subject guide (Vogel and Green, 2005). They are more easily updated and stay more current. The RSS feeds created from these subject blogs can be posted on course webpages to alert the class to new resources available (Figure 2.2).

- *Have faculty post on useful resources.* Faculty members can provide some of their most useful resources to the subject blog. This can be accomplished by commenting on databases recommended by the librarian or by posting their own list of resources on the blog.

- *Use a blog to answer frequently asked questions.* There are always those questions that are asked in every class or at the circulation desk over and over again. A blog can be used to answer such questions. By creating a category for

Figure 2.2 Hosted-online versus locally installed blogs

FAQs, a user can easily look to find what questions have been answered before asking it again.

- *Use a blog to teach searching techniques and tips.* After an in-class presentation on searching, a blog can let your students know of more techniques or tips on searching a particular database. With the reply feature of a blog, students can help each other by commenting or providing their own tips and tricks they found useful when searching. You might even learn a new tip yourself!

- *Proactively view blogs for possible opportunities to teach/help.* Brian Mathews from Georgia Tech University recently published the results of a study he did on reading student blogs. He created an account and would comment when the students mentioned being frustrated with doing research or noted needing help. He found the students very receptive and learned what perceptions they had of the library (Mathews, 2006: 2–4). This is an untapped potential for libraries.

Factors to consider

While blogs can be a useful tool in teaching and learning, keeping the blog relevant, useful and updated is important. Educators should factor in the staff time needed to post to the blog. There is nothing worse than building an audience for your blog and then not posting for several weeks. If you feel you or your staff cannot devote time each week to creating blog entries, you may be better off not starting a blog in the first place.

Wikis

Wikis (pronounced wee-kee or wick-ey per Ward Cunningham's etymology discussion on WikiWikiWeb; Cunningham, 2006a), like blogs, are websites where visitors can not only read content but also add their own content or edit the content added by others through a web browser. Both wikis and blogs are web technologies that greatly reduce technical barriers to web content creation. Both provide an editable and interactive web environment where visitors can easily create and contribute online. The broadly accessible, readable and writable web environment that blogs and wikis provide comes closer to Tim Berners-Lee's original idea for the World Wide Web (Lawson, 2005).

While both are online writing spaces, wikis differ from blogs in how visitors interact with existing content and how the two spaces organise and present added information. These differences in turn influence the ways in which blogs and wikis are used. While blog sites consist of chronologically ordered dialogues of written exchanges or 'posts' between the blog author and its visitors, wiki sites are a collection of interlinked topical pages that any (or if a restricted wiki, any authorised) visitor can quickly and easily create, expand, revise and link together. While blog visitors 'comment' in response to existing posts, wiki visitors 'edit' existing content directly. These defining structural and operational characteristics, as well as other functional features, distinguish wikis from blogs and other interactive web software (Morgan, 2006; Klobas, 2006: 6–7) and make them ideal frameworks for collaborative writing, information management and document creation. A popular wiki that you may be familiar with is Wikipedia, an online encyclopedia launched in 2001 and available for reading and editing by registered visitors (www.wikipedia.org). It is the best-known public wiki on the web today. The English-language version contains over 1,451,000 articles as of October 2006 and multiple language versions are available. As an online encyclopedia, Wikipedia illustrates the use of a wiki as an information resource that is collaboratively written by self-selected editors. While the authority and accuracy of such a publicly edited resource continue to be debated (Giles, 2005), Wikipedia is nonetheless a seminal example of the flexible, simple and collaborative writing and information management environment that a wiki provides.

Short wiki history

The term 'wiki' refers not only to a website but also to the underlying software or engine used to create, operate and maintain the wiki site. Ward Cunningham, an Oregon-based software engineer, developed the first wiki software in 1995 to enable Portland Pattern Repository programmers to work together on software code and publish it quickly. He called this new software system WikiWikiWeb (http://c2.com/cgi/wiki), a name derived from the Hawaiian word *wikiwiki* for 'speedy' or 'quick' (Leuf and Cunningham, 2001: 14–15). Cunningham's original wiki is still in use today and his wiki concept and design principles (Cunningham, 2006b) have inspired the development of numerous wiki clones (software applications that do the same thing) for different platforms and with additional features to meet specific needs.

For a more extensive definition and history of wikis, see the wiki entry on Wikipedia (http://en.wikipedia.org/wiki/ Wiki; Figure 2.3). For a list of wiki clones see the following entries on Cunningham's WikiWikiWeb and on Wikipedia:

- Jean Jordaan's list of wiki clones (http://c2.com/w4/ wikibase/?LongListOfWikiClones)

- Oscar Nierstrasz's list of wiki clones (http://c2.com/cgi/ wiki?WikiWikiClones)

- wiki software from Wikipedia (http://en.wikipedia.org/ wiki/Category:Wiki_software).

Wiki features

Wikis typically include the following features.

Figure 2.3   Wikipedia online encyclopedia entry for 'wiki'

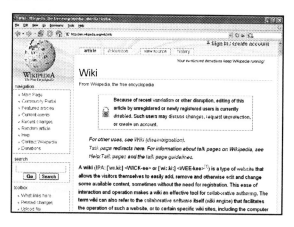

- *Page or article*. A wiki page or article is the basic unit of a wiki. A given page or article in a wiki typically covers a specific topic and contains links to other pages in the wiki as well as links to web content outside the wiki.

- *Easy webpage and link creation*. A defining characteristic of wikis is the ease with which content pages can be created and subsequently modified via a web browser. New pages are typically created by editing an existing page and adding a word, phrase or some flexible combination of characters, letters, numbers and punctuation surrounded by brackets, e.g. (my new page #1), to that page. When saved, the word appears as a hyperlink followed by a question mark (?) in the existing page. The question mark in this link indicates that it has no content behind it yet. You can then select the new link with the question mark to bring up a blank edit form and add new content for the new page there. Once saved the new page becomes part of the wiki. This 'free linking' process (www.usemod.com/cgi-bin/mb.pl?FreeLink) can be used not only to create and link to new content but also to link to existing wiki pages, external webpages, locally stored files and e-mail addresses. Originally wiki engines used words in CamelCase format for creating links: words in a phrase were joined together with the first letter of each word capitalised (e.g. MyNewPage). While CamelCase is still supported in many wikis, free linking has come into common use because of the flexibility it offers in naming wiki pages. In addition to new page creation via free linking and/or CamelCase links, many wikis also provide an easy-to-use button or link within the software for adding a new page.

- *Text markup*. Not only do wikis make the creation of links and new webpages easy, most wikis also use a simple markup syntax for formatting the content text. No knowledge of HTML markup is required, though some wikis do support use of HTML tags if desired. All wikis have simple markup conventions for common text styles and formatting such as bold, italics, underline, headings, bulleted and numbered lists and new paragraphs. Advanced wiki engines also have markup syntax for specialised features and styles such as table structures, mathematical expressions and references. Newer wikis often offer a graphical user interface within the edit function for formatting text (e.g. EditMe wiki, SeedWiki).

- *Edit function.* This is a core functional characteristic of wikis which enables any wiki visitor to create or revise its content. Open, collective editing by all visitors is the wiki default and additions or updates made by visitors are not reviewed prior to publication in the wiki. Some wikis require that editors register so that all changes are associated with the individual who made them. Also, some wikis provide *permission structures* to enable edit or write access to be limited to a defined set of users as desired. Once edited and saved, changes are immediately visible on the revised wiki pages.

- *Permission structures.* Wiki permission structures vary in the degree of granularity and control provided. Some provide a site-wide password feature which enables wiki managers to limit edit permissions on the site to a discrete group who know the password. Other wiki software enables edit permissions to be assigned at the level of specific editors and pages. Wikis software may also include a feature that enables locking specific pages from editing altogether. Pages frequently subject to spam or other disruptions can be locked to prevent these attacks.

- *Recent changes.* This list of changed pages is retained automatically by most wikis and allows wiki visitors to see what has been last changed. Some wikis support e-mail notification or RSS feeds (see next section) to alert interested visitors about page additions, changes and deletions.

- *Revision history*. Revision history, version history, page history or history is a key feature of a wiki that tracks all the edits and versions for a given wiki page (Figure 2.4). As discussed by the WikiMatrix page history section (www.wikimatrix.org/wiki/feature:page_history), revision history is implemented differently in different wiki software; however, essential components include a record of the date and time an edit occurred, the IP address or logged-in username of the visitor who made the change and, most importantly, a link to previous versions of the page which allows restoration of those versions and makes all wiki edits reversible. This previous version restoration feature is critical, particularly in a fully open wiki, in order to recover from unintentional errors, edit wars and the inevitable and often malicious spam.

- *Discussion pages*. Discussion, comment or talk pages are areas for each page within the wiki where visitors can ask

Figure 2.4 Revision history for WikiHome page in the Jotspot Wiki

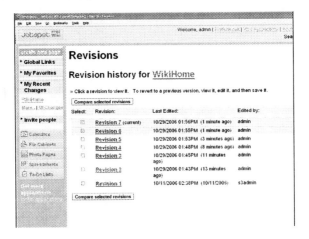

questions or discuss the page content with others. Where editors have differing opinions about an article's content, discussion pages provide a space to discuss and resolve issues in lieu of conducting back-and-forth editing of the public content (commonly referred to as an 'edit war').

- *Search function.* Most wikis include a simple keyword search engine that enables searching editable wiki content. Some wikis (e.g. PmWiki, TWiki) have more advanced search functionality including Boolean logic, phrase searching, results ordering and the ability to target searches at specific pages or groups of pages. Some wikis can also search documents uploaded to the wiki such as Word or PDF files.

- *Security/anti-spam.* In addition to access restriction features discussed under permissions structures above, some wikis (e.g. EditMe, TWiki, MediaWiki, Confluence) include features such as CAPTCHAs and/or spam blacklists to protect against vandalism by automated spamming bots and from known spam URLs. With spam becoming an increasingly common problem for web-based systems, these and other anti-spam features can save significant site maintenance time spent in repeated restoration of last versions of pages to replace the spam-ridden versions.

Other features

Some other useful features to consider when selecting wiki software include the following.

- *Backlinks.* Backlinks is a view of all wiki pages that link to the currently displayed page.

- *File uploads.* Many wikis provide a mechanism for uploading MS Word, PDF, image, sound and other files for linking in wiki pages. For security and space conservation, wiki managers can limit the types and sizes of files that can be uploaded.

- *Hierarchical organisation.* More advanced wiki software (e.g. Jotspot, PmWiki. TWiki, MediaWiki) provides a way for editors to organise wiki pages into one or more hierarchical categories. These page relationships are often then displayed in breadcrumb navigation on the pages.

- *Blikis.* Some blogs now include wiki functionality to enable bloggers to edit their initial posts and make blogging more interactive. These combined blog/wiki systems are also called blickis or wikilogs among other names. Further discussion of blikis may be found in the bliki entry on Wikipedia (http://en.wikipedia.org/wiki/Bliki).

Wiki engines vary in their implementation of these and other features. Enterprise wikis such as Confluence, Socialtext and TWiki are designed for organisational use and require different and more advanced functionality than those designed for individual or smaller group use. Enterprise wiki feature implementations include robust permission structures, advanced search and user management to enable organisations to share and manage information securely. Some of these enterprise-class wiki engines (e.g. TWiki, Confluence, Jotspot) also provide a powerful plug-in architecture to enable addition or development of applications within the wiki to support business processes such as calendaring, calculations and charting and project tracking and management.

Creating a wiki

To create your own wiki you must first select a wiki engine to use. As with blogs, wiki engines are available as online-hosted systems managed by others or as software packages that can be downloaded, installed on a local server and

Figure 2.5   EditMe, an online-hosted wiki system

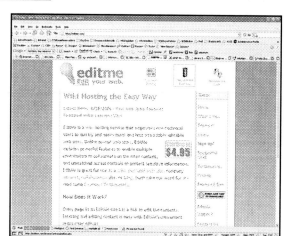

administered by your organisation's technical staff. Some hosted systems require a subscription fee (e.g. EditMe); others are free to set up a small, basic wiki and incur a fee to host a wiki with greater space requirements or advanced functionality (e.g. Jotspot, PBWiki).

Online hosting offers a quick and easy way to create a wiki. For librarians and educators who want to get their wiki up and running immediately or whose organisations are not able to host and support a local wiki installation, an online-hosted system is a great solution. Some examples are PBWiki, SeedWiki, Jotspot and EditMe (Figure 2.5). SocialText is another online-hosted solution targeted at business and other enterprise environments.

Many wiki systems available for local installation are free and open source (e.g. CanvasWiki, TWiki, PmWiki, MediaWiki); others charge a subscription fee (e.g. Confluence). The system can be used as is or enhanced by local web developers as desired. For ease of support and development, it is best to select wiki software written in

Figure 2.6   MediaWiki wiki software download page

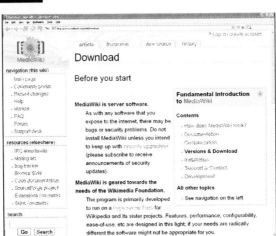

a programming language supported by your systems development staff and infrastructure. A locally installed and administered wiki engine can provide a level of flexibility and customisation not available in hosted online systems. IT support for system administration, software support and enhancement are key considerations.

MediaWiki (Figure 2.6), the wiki engine behind Wikipedia, is free, open source and available for download and local installation (www.mediawiki.org/wiki/MediaWiki).

There are advantages and disadvantages to both online-hosted and locally installed wiki systems. Key considerations are summarised in Table 2.2.

In selecting your wiki engine, whether an online-hosted service or locally installed, consider the wiki features needed and assess the costs and benefits of the various wiki systems in terms of your budget, staff resources, technical expertise, implementation complexity and flexibility.

An invaluable web resource to assist you in the wiki engine selection process is the WikiMatrix wiki comparison site (http://wikimatrix.org). This website provides extensive

Table 2.2   Online-hosted versus locally installed wikis

	Advantages	Disadvantages
Hosted online	No software installation Can be up and running in a day Updates and maintenance are handled by host service Security is handled by host service	Separate address from your library website Less flexibility on features Site may disappear or charge for their services in the future There may be a subscription cost to use advanced features or when wiki grows beyond a certain size
Locally installed	More control over the wiki function and look and feel More flexible solution for multiple wikis Often free and open source	Must install software Responsibility for updates and maintenance Responsibility for security and software Requires more technical knowledge Takes more than a day to implement

information on various hosted and locally installed wiki engines and has a selection wizard and comparison tool which allows you to select and compare these engines based on their features. Other helpful wiki directories can be found on the WikiWikiWeb and Wikipedia websites:

- *locally installed wiki engines*

    http://c2.com/cgi/wiki?WikiChoiceTree
    http://en.wikipedia.org/wiki/List_of_wiki_software

- *wiki online hosting services*

    http://c2.com/cgi/wiki?WikiFarms

    http://en.wikipedia.org/wiki/List_of_wiki_farms.

Should you decide to implement a wiki engine on your local library network, helpful technical documentation may be found on the particular wiki engine website. Some of the available books on wikis (Ebersbach et al., 2006; Leuf and Cunningham, 2001) are also good sources of technical information.

Wiki uses in libraries and education

In academic environments, librarians and educators are using wikis in a variety of ways. The flexible, collaborative writing spaces that wikis create introduce new opportunities for engaging and collaborating with students and library patrons as well as within providing group writing space for committees, communities of practice, and research or project teams. As Klobas (2006: 14) and fellow contributors illustrate, 'wikis are "social information spaces"' as initially defined and described by Fisher (2003). While wikis can certainly be used by one person as a web-accessible personal information space, the more interesting uses leverage the collaborative features of wikis. Below is a sampling of actual and potential wiki uses in libraries and education.

Subject guides

Wikis provide a useful, quick and low-tech way to create and maintain web-based library subject guides. Librarians have historically created subject guides for the web via standard web editors and then forwarded these to their website manager for posting on the library website. With a wiki, library staff can create subject guides in real time with the novel advantage of enabling colleagues and interested visitors not only to comment on the guides (as a blog would also allow) but also contribute material to them. Chad Boeninger's BizWiki guide to business resources at Ohio State University (www.library.ohiou.edu/subjects/bizwiki/ index. php/Main_Page) is an often-cited example of a wiki-based subject guide: it is an open wiki site that faculty, staff, students and other visitors can edit once they have registered.

Conference planning

Wikis are increasing used for conference planning in library and information science and higher education. A wiki provides a shared information space where international or otherwise distributed conference planners and participants can share information with all conference attendees. Typically, conference organisers will seed the wiki with initial information about the conference programme and location and other attendees add information and recommendations on dining, hotels, transportation, places to see in the conference city, free WiFi locations and social events, among other topics. Example conference planning wikis include the Internet Librarian 2006 wiki (http://il2006.pbwiki.com/), an online-hosted wiki, and the ASIST 2006 Annual Meeting Wiki (www.asis.org/wiki/AM06/index.php/Main_Page), a locally installed wiki. A comparable example from higher education is the 2007 HigherEd BlogCon planning wiki (http://higheredblogcon. editme.com/).

Documents and knowledge bases

A wiki can provide an ideal tool and information space for creating and maintaining collaboratively prepared documents of all kinds. Some natural wiki candidates in libraries and academic settings include policies; procedure manuals; topical glossaries or encyclopedias; reference or general library FAQs; best practice collections; technical documentation; student or faculty project notebooks; committee agendas, minutes and reports; and research documents and articles. Any document or knowledge base that would benefit from, if not require, quick and easy access, input and updates by multiple collaborators would be well suited to a wiki. A well-known best practice collection example from the library domain is Meridith Farkas's Library Success: A Best Practices Wiki (www.libsuccess.org/), which provides a central location for the library community to document and share ideas and successful library endeavours of all kinds. Klobas (2006: 78–94; 124–38) describes this and a number of other useful collaborative knowledge-base-type wikis created by and for information professionals and educators.

Collaborative writing

A common use of wikis in the academic setting is to support collaborative writing among students and faculty. For students, wikis are used and supported as a pedagogically beneficial platform for instructing them in the writing process (Lamb, 2004: 44–5; Mitchell, 2006: 132–3). For faculty researchers and teachers, wikis provide an efficient online writing tool for collaborative preparation of research papers and curriculum materials (Mitchell, 2006: 133–5). Such collaborative writing wiki environments may be restricted to authors only to provide a protected environment for student writing and unpublished research material.

Commentable library catalogue

The OCLC is integrating wiki functionality into Open WorldCat to allow web catalogue users and non-cataloguing librarians to contribute content to information resource records. Catalogue users can set up an account and then add notes, ratings and critiques in certain portions of the record. The OCLC provides guidelines and monitors the submissions. For a description of system features, see www.oclc.org/worldcat/web/features/.

Intranet/website content management

As discussed earlier, wikis range from lightweight to robust in their implementations. Those, like enterprise wikis mentioned earlier, on the robust end of the spectrum are essentially content management systems. Depending on institutional needs, libraries and academic units may wish to review these wiki engines along with traditional content management systems for use in managing content in both public and intranet web systems. Wikipedia provides an overview comparison of wikis and more traditional content management systems (http://en.wikipedia.org/wiki/Wiki# Wikis_and_content_management_systems).

Some factors in wiki success

Wikis provide an attractive platform for engaging students and library users and supporting collaboration among and with them. However, setting up a wiki system is only the first step and cannot ensure that people will visit or contribute to the wiki. The following factors are important to optimise the chances of a wiki's success.

- Identify specific goals for the wiki. In conjunction with those goals, determine who the authors and collaborators will be and if some audiences will only need to read the wiki or if the wiki will be open to editing by all visitors. Configure wiki access permissions as needed to support these decisions.

- Establish policies and guidelines for wiki use and include them within the wiki for easy reference. Provide hands-on training in wiki use, if possible.

- Select staff to monitor changes to the wiki and watch for spam and edit wars. Use RSS feeds to facilitate and as appropriate distribute the monitoring process.

- Seed the wiki with initial organisation and content to establish a framework that wiki authors can refer to and build upon. A substantial base of organisation categories and content helps overcome the hesitation new wiki authors may have in using this tool and the inertia created by an empty wiki.

- Consider using a wiki that has a WYSIWYG interface so that non-technical users are able to create wiki content just as easily as they do a word processing document.

- Use the wiki appropriately. Wikis at this point are primarily text-based tools. If mapping or visualisation tools are more appropriate to the task at hand, use the most helpful tool; do not use the wiki just because it is there.

- To ensure the best collaborative experience with the wiki, ensure that the wiki engine supports concurrent editing so that one author's changes do not overwrite another author's changes.

- To ensure spam does not become a maintenance burden for an open-access wiki, ensure the wiki software has spam management tools and the ability to lock pages from editing altogether.

- To ensure the ability to use and move wiki content easily to other systems or formats, verify the information storage, management and export capabilities of the wiki system.

- Promote the wiki. An excellent way to spark interest of library staff and patrons in the wiki is to seed it right away with a tool or resource of interest to them. For library staff this might include using it to host subject guides or as a workspace for conference paper writing with colleagues. Student users could be introduced to the wiki as part of library instruction courses by hosting instructional materials and interactive question sets there.

RSS

The term RSS has three different meanings according to who you ask. The acronym itself can stand for RDF (resource document framework) site summary, rich site summary or real simple syndication. RSS uses an XML-formatted file to push content to subscribers. Each time the RSS file is updated, the subscriber is notified that new content is available for viewing.

Before 2005 blogs were the main application using RSS. Most blogging software incorporated some mechanism for creating an RSS feed. Since 2005 the use of RSS has expanded (Figure 2.7) to include:

■ notifying subscribers of new podcast episodes;

Figure 2.7 Versions of RSS and their uses

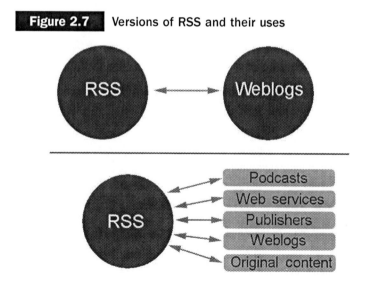

- showing the table of contents for new journals direct from the publishers;

- retrieving search results from databases via a defined search strategy;

- delivering original content from websites.

There are currently eight versions of RSS in use today. Each version is an improvement on the previous one. This discussion will highlight the three most popular versions of RSS and their features.

- 0.91 (http://my.netscape.com/publish/formats/rss-spec-0.91.html). Developed by UserLand (www.userland.com/), it is used for basic syndication. It is still widely popular because of its simplicity.

- 1.0 (http://web.resource.org/rss/1.0/spec). Developed to conform to the W3C's RDF framework, this version allows for more sophisticated metadata to be added to the feed. This version is recommended by the MedBiquitous Consortium, a group founded by Johns Hopkins Medicine to advance healthcare education through standards (www.medbiq.org/technology/tech_architecture/rssguidelines.pdf), for use by publishers since it can incorporate more complex metadata in the feed.

- 2.0 (http://blogs.law.harvard.edu/tech/rss). Dave Winer, the developer of RSS 0.91, also developed this version. It expanded the size of some of the RSS fields. RSS 2.0 is used by podcasters to syndicate their feeds.

RSS is not the only game in town. There are three other syndication frameworks on the internet.

- Atom (www.atomenabled.org/). Created by leading service providers, tool vendors and independent developers, Atom

46

is designed to be a universal publishing standard for personal content and weblogs. The standard allows for more complex information to be inserted into the feed. It is also more consistent in its appearance across syndication.

- OPML (Outline Processor Markup Language – www.opml .org/). As the name implies, this XML-based format is designed to syndicate outlined structured data. OPML can be used to push several RSS feeds at one time.

- SSE (Simple Sharing Extensions – http://msdn.microsoft. com/xml/rss/sse/). Developed by Microsoft, these extensions are 'used in conjunction with RSS and OPML to define the minimum extensions necessary to enable loosely-cooperating apps'. SSE is still under development.

The type of feed format you use (Table 2.3) will rely heavily on the type of content you will be syndicating.

Creating RSS feeds

RSS feeds can be created in a variety of ways.

- If you are using a blog, most blogging software will automatically create the RSS feed for you.

- RSS feeds can be created from queries to a database, such as an electronic resources database or library catalogue. Many of the ILS vendors are starting to create RSS feeds for new acquisitions or reading lists.

- Knowing a little HTML, you can create a feed yourself with just a text editor and the basic structure of an RSS feed.

- There are programs such as FeedForAll (www. feedforall.com/) which provide a simple form to fill out for each item in the feed. It then creates the XML file for you.

Table 2.3 Basic structures of RSS, Atom and OPML feeds

RSS 0.91	Atom 1.0	OPML 1.0
<rss version="0.91">	<?xml version="1.0"	<opml>
<channel>	encoding="utf-8" ?>	<head>
<image>	<feed	<title> ...</title>
<item>	xmlns="http://www.w3.org/	</head>
<title> ... </title>	2005/Atom">	
<link> ...</link>	<title> ... </title>	<body>
<description>...		<outline type="rss"
</description>	<link href="http://....../>	title="..." url="...">
</item>	<updated>...</updated>	<outline text="..."
<item>	<author>	type="..." f="...">
<title> ... </title>	<name> ...</name>	<outline text="..."
<link> ... </link>	</author>	type="..."
<description>...	<id> ... </id>	isComment="true|false"
</description>		IsBreakpoint="true|
</item>	<entry>	false">
.....	<title> ... </title>	</body>
</channel>	<link href="http://...>	</opml>
</rss>	<id> ...</id>	
	<updated> ...</updated>	
	<summary> ...	
	</summary>	
	</entry>	
	</feed>	

Once you have your XML file, you will need to alert users to the feed. Within the HTML of your page, add the following code:

- <link rel="alternate" type="application/rss+xml" title=" "href="http://yoursite/xmlfilename" /> for RSS;

- <link rel="alternate" type="application/atom+xml" title=" "href="http://yoursite/xmlfilename" /> for Atom.

When patrons visit your page, their browser will alert them that an RSS feed is available. There are several icons, also called chicklets, that can be used to note an RSS feed is available (Figure 2.8). The two most commonly used are

Figure 2.8 RSS feed icons

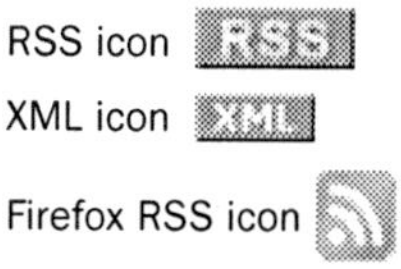

RSS icon RSS
XML icon XML

Firefox RSS icon

RSS and XML. The Firefox RSS icon has been chosen as the industry standard icon for RSS feeds (www.feedicons. com/).

Newsreaders/aggregators

The XML file that makes up the RSS feed is not easily readable by the human eye. The file is meant to be read using a newsreader or aggregator. There are many types of aggregators available.

- *Web-based*. These aggregators are useful for individuals who want to keep up with news wherever they go.
  - Bloglines (www.bloglines.com/)
  - MyYahoo (http://my.yahoo.com/)
- *Desktop software*. These applications can be freeware, shareware or commercial programs.
  - FeedReader (www.feedreader.com/)
  - FeedDemon (www.feeddemon.com/)
- *Web browser add-ons/extensions*. Extensions add additional functionality to a browser.
  - Sage (http://sage.mozdev.org/)
  - Pluck (www.pluck.com/)
  - Safari (www.apple.com/macosx/features/safari/)

- *E-mail client readers*. Like a browser extension, e-mail RSS readers add this functionality to the e-mail client.
  - Mozilla Thunderbird (www.mozilla.com/thunderbird/)
  - Attensa (www.attensa.com/)
- *Palm/pocket PC/cell phone software*. Programs developed specifically for these mobile devices.
  - PocketRSS(www.happyjackroad.net/pocketpc/pocketRSS/pocketRSS.asp)
  - AvantGo (www.avantgo.com/)

Aggregators are used to subscribe to the feed, view a listing of items within the feed and read those items of interest. The feed leads the subscriber to the content on the provider's website.

RSS capabilities in integrated library systems

Integrated library systems (ILS) have been slow to incorporate RSS into their online catalogue systems. Table 2.4 gives some information on how the top three ILS vendors are incorporating RSS feeds. Endeavor, another top ILS, does not have RSS capabilities or does not note that it is available on its website. Information was pulled from press releases from the companies and by visiting sites using the software. Unfortunately, these vendors do not list the specifics on their RSS features on their sites.

Research implications of RSS

Pulling together various information resources, especially on the internet, can be a daunting task. Researchers are

Table 2.4	Top ILS vendors incorporating RSS feeds		
	SirsiDynix	ExLibris	Innovative Interfaces
RSS capable	Yes	Yes	Yes
Product	Enterprise Portal Solution Sirsi Rooms 2.0	ALEPH 500 Version 18	Millennium 2006LE WebPAC Pro
User-created RSS feeds	Yes – from all searchable sources	Yes – from OPAC ExLibris supports OpenSearch RSS, a standard that allows searching of library catalogues from search engines such as A9.com and creating an RSS feed from them	Not clear – the press release is vague; it does not sound as though the user can create a feed from an OPAC search A look at one of its beta sites does not have this feature included
Librarian-created RSS feeds	Yes	Yes	Yes – through Millennium Feed Builder
RSS feeds for patron information	Yes	Not clear from press release	Yes – the patron can receive information on placed holds and availability of items via an RSS feed
Outside RSS feed integration	Yes	Yes	Yes

finding RSS feeds to be a valuable research tool. Pulling RSS feeds from OPACs, journals, news feeds and blogs on a specific research subject can cut research time down considerably. Librarians can help in creating feeds on subject areas or by instructing patrons on how to use RSS feeds and where to find reliable/authoritative feeds to use in their research.

Using RSS in teaching

- *News outlet.* Push the latest information about the library, its events or new resources to interested individuals. If you pull this information from a blog, put the RSS feed on the homepage as a quick way to see the latest happenings at the library!
- *Current awareness/SDI tool.* Databases such as PubMed and ProQuest are making searches available as an RSS feed. Create a feed that highlights local authors' works or tie a complicated search to a course webpage or blog to help students.
- *Subject guide feed.* Create a feed to go along with a professor's blog for a course. The RSS feed can be incorporated in the blog and list new resources, searching tips or news items of interest to the class.

Podcasts

iPod + broadcast = podcast.
Podcasts owe their name to former MTV VJ Adam Curry. He coined the term by taking the most popular portable audio device and melding it with broadcast.

What is a podcast and how do I subscribe?

Podcasts are simply audio files. So what makes them unique? Let us put it into perspective. Much like deciding what magazine you want to subscribe to and sending in your request, you select podcasts to subscribe to using an aggregator such as iTunes or iPodder. Podcasts are created usually on a schedule, and when a new podcast is created it is sent to your aggregator, just like a new issue of a magazine is sent to your home. You can listen to the podcast on your computer or take it with you on your portable audio device. These audio files are usually in the MP3 format. If you do not like the podcast or your tastes change, you can just unsubscribe to the feed. You will still have the files that have already been downloaded and can keep or delete them at your leisure. The best thing about podcasts that makes them very different from magazines is that the majority of podcasts are free!

iPod required?

One of the fundamental questions about podcasting is if an iPod is required. As noted above, any device that can play an MP3 file can play a podcast. A recent study by Bridge Data (Dixon and Greeson, 2006) notes that more than 80 per cent of podcasts never make it on to an iPod or any other portable audio device: most are listened to on a computer or never listened to at all. While portability is seen as the biggest benefit of podcasts, it is not necessarily the main feature.

The iPod and other portable audio devices have become quite prevalent. According to an April 2005 Pew Internet & American Life Project study, more than 22 million American adults own either an iPod or another MP3 player. Of this 22 million, 29 per cent have listened to podcasts and at least 35 per cent are under the age of 40 (Rainie and Madden, 2005: 1)

In 2006 Student Monitor, a marketing research firm, did its biannual survey of undergraduate college students. As reported in the *Washington Post* of 8 June 2006, 73 per cent of the students surveyed put the iPod at the top of their list of most popular items (*Washington Post*, 2006). In the prior survey it only received 59 per cent of votes. This is the first time since 1997 that beer was not the most popular item, adding to the 'in' status of the iPod among students.

Types of podcasts and their creation

Podcasts come in three flavours: audio, video and enhanced. Each has its own unique creation methodology.

To create an audio podcast, the basic set-up consists of a hand-held microphone, a digital recorder (either a computer or portable voice recorder), headphones and audio editing software. You can record the podcast directly on the computer or use a portable voice recorder to record the audio, then download it to a computer. A freeware program, Audacity (http://audacity.sourceforge.net/), can be used to record and edit the audio.

There are many programs available to help create a podcast: a listing can be found at www.podcastingnews. com/topics/Podcasting_Software.html. Want music in your podcast? There are podcast-safe music sites on the internet; a listing can be found at www.podcastingnews.com/topics/ Podcast-Legal_Music.html.

Screencasting, vidcasting or enhanced podcast?

With the debut of the Video iPod in 2005, vidcasts or VODcasts (video on demand) have become popular. Along with vidcasts, screencasts and enhanced podcasts provide visual information as well as aural.

Vidcasting

Vidcasts are created using a video camera (digital camera preferred). They can then be edited with QuickTime Pro (http://developer.apple.com/quicktime/) or Final Cut Pro (www.apple.com/finalcutstudio/finalcutpro/). These two programs have the option to save a file in an iPod-compatible format – usually .mov or .mp4 format.

Screencasting

Screencasts differ from vidcasts in that they are partly or wholly a computer screen with audio commentary to describe the action on the computer screen. Vidcasts usually involve some type of live action. They can be created using programs such as Camtasia (www.techsmith.com/ camtasia.asp) or Snapz Pro X (Mac) (www.ambrosiasw. com/utilities/snapzprox/).

Enhanced podcasts

Enhanced podcasts incorporate slides, pdfs, websites and images with audio. They use the AAC (Advanced Audio Coding) format with extra scripting to bring up the visual image or website (Figure 2.9). Programs available for

Figure 2.9   Viewing an enhanced podcast via iTunes

creating enhanced podcasts include Camtasia, Windows Media File Editor (www.microsoft.com/windows/windowsmedia/forpros/encoder/utilities.aspx) and ProfCast (www.profcast.com). ProfCast requires the Mac OS to operate and works in conjunction with the iLife (www.apple.com/ilife/) package available with Mac OS 10.

Once the file is created, it will need to be uploaded to a server. An RSS feed is then created to notify users of the podcast's availability. For podcasts, RSS version 2.0 has the necessary coding for the audio file (Table 2.5). RSS 2.0 works for all types of podcasts. You can then promote your podcast to the various search engines and to iTunes.

Podcasts versus streaming audio

Many websites use streaming audio to present events or instruction. Are podcasts a better avenue for these types of presentations? Table 2.6 looks at the differences between podcasts and streaming audio. Both have a place in instruction and presentations.

iTunes University

In 2006 Apple announced plans for iTunes University (www.apple.com/education/solutions/itunes_u/). This service would initially work with 200 selected colleges and universities to create educational content for the iPod and provide a place to access these materials through iTunes. Professors could hide content behind an ID/password system tied to the campus authentication system on a class-by-class basis. This content, sometimes called coursecasting, grew out of trials done by Stanford and Duke in 2004–2005.

Apple has stated it will provide any institution interested in being part of this two-year trial of iTunes University with

Table 2.5 Basic RSS 2.0 feed

```
<?xml version="1.0" encoding="UTF-8"?>
<rss version="2.0">
<channel>
<lastBuildDate>Mon, 10 Apr 2006 21:02:44-0700</last
  BuildDate>
<title>...</title>
<link>...</link>
 <description>...</description>
<language>en</language>
<copyright>...</copyright>
<image>
   <url>...</url>
    <title>...</title>
    <link>...</link>
     <width></width>
     <height></height>
</image>
<category>...</category>
<item>
 <title>...</title>
  <description>...</description>
   <enclosure type="audio/mpeg" url="filename.mp3"
   length="15181178"/>
  <guid>filename.mp3</guid>
<pubDate>Mon, 10 Apr 2006 20:50:37 -
0700</pubDate>
<category>...</category>
</item>
</channel>
</rss>
```

Table 2.6   Podcasts versus streaming audio

Streaming audio	Podcasts
Requires the user to be on the internet to listen	Can be played on the computer or on a portable audio player
Can be used to broadcast live events	Come already in an archived format
Can be recorded and archived	Come directly to user via an RSS feed
Access only one stream at a time	Can download several feeds at a time

a terabyte of storage space and pay for the bandwidth. Apple will also provide training on the iLife suite of programs that can help in the creation of podcasts, vidcasts and enhanced podcasts.

What could this mean for the library? Libraries can take advantage of the movement to develop podcasts, vidcasts and enhanced podcasts that can be used by students and the public at large. Library staff can attend the classes on using iLife and pass that knowledge on to others. Classes on how to subscribe to podcasts via iTunes would need to be offered for those who do not already use it.

Podcasting applications in teaching

- *Audio or video tours of the library.* Create a podcast or vidcast to help patrons find their way around your library. These tours could be tailored towards specific groups.

- *Reinforce searching techniques.* Teaching database searching skills is an everyday occurrence in libraries. By using a vidcast, screencast or enhanced podcast, patrons can get help on searching even when the library is closed.

- *Create how-to-search modules.* Create a screencast showing the features or advanced techniques for searching databases or the online catalogue.

- *Record special events/lectures in the library.* Many libraries offer lecture series or other special events throughout the year. Creating a podcast of an event makes it available for those who could not attend and publicises future events.

- *Provide materials for distance education students.* Distance learning has boomed in the past few years. Libraries are aware of the need for resources for these non-traditional students. Podcasts or vidcasts can be tailored specifically for these students to help then in using the library's website or accessing materials from off campus.

References

Bausch, P., Haughey, M. and Hourihan, M. (2002) *We Blog: Publishing Online with Weblogs*. Indianapolis, IN: Wiley.

Casey, Michael E. and Savastinuk, Laura C. (2006) 'Library 2.0', *Library Journal*, 131: 40–2.

Cunningham, Ward (2006a) 'Correspondence on the etymology of wiki'; available at: *http://c2.com/doc/etymology.html* (accessed: 30 September 2006).

Cunningham, Ward (2006b) 'Wiki design principles'; available at: *http://c2.com/cgi/wiki?WikiDesignPrinciples* (accessed: 4 October 2006).

Dixon, C. and Greeson, M. (2006) 'Recasting the concept of podcasting: Part I', 23 March; available at *http://news.digitaltrends.com/talkback109.html* (accessed: 20 April 2006).

Ebersbach, Anja, Glaser, Marcus and Heigl, Richard (2006) *Wiki: Web Collaboration*. Berlin: Springer-Verlag.

Fisher, D. (2003) 'Studying social information spaces', in C. Leug and D. Fisher (eds) *From Usenet to CoWebs*. London: Springer-Verlag, pp. 3–19.

Giles, Jim (2005) 'Internet encyclopedias go head to head', 14 December; available at: *www.nature.com/news/2005/051212/pf/438900a_pf.html* (accessed: 28 March 2006).

Klobas, Jane (2006) *Wikis: Tools for Information Work and Collaboration*. Oxford: Chandos Publishing.

Lamb, B. (2004) 'Wide open spaces ready or not', *EDUCAUSE Review*, September/October: 36–48.

Lawson, Mark (2005) 'Berners-Lee on the read/write web', interview with Tim Berners-Lee, BBC News, 9 August; available at: *http://news.bbc.co.uk/2/hi/technology/4132752.stm* (accessed: 9 August 2005).

Leuf, Bo and Cunningham, Ward (2001) *The Wiki Way: Quick Collaboration on the Web*. Boston, MA: Addison-Wesley.

Mathews, Brian (2006) 'Intuitive revelations: the ubiquitous reference model', Georgia Institute of Technology; available at: *http://hdl.handle.net/1853/8446* (accessed: 20 April 2006).

Mitchell, Pru (2006) 'Wikis in education', in Jane Klobas *Wikis: Tools for Information Work and Collaboration*. Oxford: Chandos Publishing, 119–47.

Morgan, M.C. (2006) 'WikiAndBlog', ENGL 3177/5177 course wiki at Bemidji (MN) State University; available at: *http://199.17.178.148/~morgan/cgi-bin/blogsandwiki.pl?WikiAndBlog* (accessed: 27 August 2006).

O'Reilly, Tim (2005) 'What is Web 2.0?', 30 September; available at: *www.oreillynet.com/pub/a/oreilly/tim/news/2005/09/30/what-is-web-20.html* (accessed: 1 December 2005).

Rainie, L. and Madden, M. (2005) 'Podcasting catches on', Pew Internet & American Life Project, 3 April; available at: *www.pewinternet.org/pdfs/PIP_podcasting.pdf* (accessed: 20 April 2006).

Vogel, Teri M. and Green, Doug (2005) 'Delivering the news with blogs: the Georgia State University library experience', *Internet Reference Services Quarterly*, 10(1): 5–27.

Washington Post (2006) 'Survey: iPods more popular than beer', 8 June; available at: *www.washingtonpost.com/wp-dyn/content/article/2006/06/08/AR2006060800455.html* (accessed: 9 June 2006).

Further reading

Blansit, B. Douglas (2006) 'Using RSS to publish library news and information', *Journal of Electronic Resources in Medical Libraries*, 3: 95–103.

Blood, Rebecca (2002) *The Weblog Handbook*. Cambridge: Perseus Publishing.

Chawner, Brenda and Lewis, Paul H. (2006) 'WikiWikiWebs: new ways to communicate in a web environment', *Information Technology and Libraries*, 25(1): 33–43.

Cochrane, Todd (2005) *Podcasting: The Do-It-Yourself Guide*. Indianapolis, IN: Wiley.

EDUCAUSE Learning Initiative (2005) '7 things you should know about... podcasting', June; available at: *www.educause.edu/ir/library/pdf/ELI7003.pdf* (accessed: 9 June 2006).

EDUCAUSE Learning Initiative (2005) '7 things you should know about... videoblogging', August; available at: *www.educause.edu/ir/library/pdf/ELI7005.pdf* (accessed: 9 June 2006).

EDUCAUSE Learning Initiative (2005) '7 things you should know about... wikis', July; available at: *www.educause.edu/ir/library/pdf/ELI7004.pdf* (accessed: 20 July 2006).

EDUCAUSE Learning Initiative (2006) '7 things you should know about... Screencasting', March; available at: *www.educause.edu/ir/library/pdf/ELI7012.pdf* (accessed: 9 June 2006).

Farkas, Meridith (2005) 'So you want to build a wiki?', September; available at: *http://webjunction.org/do/DisplayContent?id=11262* (accessed: 29 October 2006).

Farkas, Meridith (2005) 'Using wikis to create online communities', September; available at: *http://webjunction.org/do/DisplayContent?id=11264* (accessed: 29 October 2006).

Finkelstein, Ellen (2005) *Syndicating Web Sites with RSS Feeds for Dummies*. Indianapolis, IN: Wiley.

Gorissen, Pierre (2005) 'Enhanced podcasts for all', 26 October; available at: *www.gorissen.info/Pierre/files/enhanced-podcasts-for-all.pdf* (accessed: 20 April 2006).

Honan, Matthew (2006) 'Libraries turning to iPods and iTunes', 13 February; available at: *http://playlistmag.com/features/2006/02/library/index.php* (accessed: 20 April 2006).

Lum, Lydia (2006) 'The power of podcasting', *Diverse Issues in Higher Education*, 23: 32–5.

Mader, Stewart (2006) 'Using wiki in education', 30 October; available at: *www.ikiw.org/* (accessed: 30 October 2006).

Martindale, Trey and Wiley, David A. (2006) 'Using weblogs in scholarship and teaching', *TechTrends*, 49: 55–61.

McElherarn, Kirk, Giles, Richard and Herrington, Jack D. (2006) *Podcasting Pocket Guide*. Sebastopol: O'Reilly.

Richardson, Will (2004) 'Blogging and RSS – the "what's it?" and "how to" of powerful new web tools for educators', *Multimedia and Internet@Schools Magazine*, 11; available at: *www.infotoday.com/MMSchools/jan04/Richardson.shtml* (accessed: 27 May 2005).

Richardson, Will (2006) *Blogs, Wikis, Podcasts, and Other Powerful Web Tools for Classrooms*. Thousand Oaks, CA: Corwin Press.

Stafford, Toma and Webb, Matt (2006) 'What is a wiki (and how to use one for your projects)', 20 July; available at: *www.oreillynet.com/pub/a/network/2006/07/07/what-is-a-wiki.html?page=2#using-a-wiki* (accessed: 2 October 2006).

Stephens, Michael (2006) 'Web 2.0 and libraries: best practices for social software', *Library Technology Reports*, 42(4): 6–68.

Tonkin, Emma (2005) 'Making a case for wiki', *ARIADNE*, 42; available at: *www.ariadne.ac.uk/issue42/tonkin/* (accessed: 30 January 2005).

Udell, Jon (2005) 'What is screencasting?', 16 Nov ember; available at: *www.oreillynet.com/lpt/a/6119* (accessed: 30 August 2006).

University of Wisconsin – Madison (2005) 'Teaching and learning with podcasting'; available at: *http://engage .doit.wisc.edu/podcasting/teachandlearn/* (accessed: 20 March 2006).

'Web_2.0, Introduction', Wikipedia; available at: http://en .wikipedia.org/wiki/Web_2.0#Introduction (accessed: 3 December 2006).

Recommended blogs

Blogging Libraries Wiki (www.blogwithoutalibrary.net/ links/index.php?title=Welcome_to_the_Blogging_ Libraries_Wiki).

David Lee King (www.davidleeking.com/).

Learning 2.0 (http://plcmclearning.blogspot.com/).

RSS4Lib (www.rss4lib.com/).

Tame the Web: Libraries and Technology (http://tametheweb .com/).

The Krafty Librarian (http://kraftylibrarian.blogspot.com/).

The Shifted Librarian – Shifting libraries at the speed of byte! (www.theshiftedlibrarian.com/).

Recommended podcasts

Arizona State University Libraries (www.asu.edu/lib/ podcasts/).

Education Podcast Network (http://epnweb.org/).

Library Audio to Go – George C. Gordon Library, Worcester Polytechnic Institute (www.wpi.edu/Academics/Library/ Borrowing/Podcasts/).

University of Sheffield Main Library iPod Induction Tour (www.lbasg.group.shef.ac.uk/downloads/mainlibrary .html).

3

Virtual reference and instruction

Amy VanScoy and Megan Oakleaf

Effective instruction in the virtual reference environment

Most academic libraries use chat technology as a complement to their established in-person, telephone and e-mail reference services. The name librarians have adopted for this technology, virtual reference or digital reference, describes the original or most comfortable use of the service – ready-reference or other short-answer questions. Since the inception of chat technology services, librarians have struggled with patrons who require one-to-one instruction to address their information needs, and this topic has recently been addressed in scholarly publications and at professional conferences. This chapter seeks to provide an overview of the instructional uses of virtual reference in academic libraries and includes strategies for using virtual reference transactions to support patron learning.

Virtual reference in academic libraries

'Virtual reference' is a phrase used to describe online reference services that allow patrons and librarians to communicate via text. Sometimes virtual reference services allow librarians and patrons to 'co-browse' or share webpages. Many academic libraries offer virtual reference to supplement their in-person, phone and e-mail reference services; however, the type and sophistication of these services vary widely, depending on the needs of a library's patrons, the amount of money a library can afford to invest and the level of technical support available to the librarians.

Some virtual reference services employ publicly available instant messaging services, including AOL Instant Messenger, MSN, Yahoo and Google Talk. These technologies allow librarians to 'chat' with patrons by typing text; the services also allow file-sharing and voice communication, but at the time of writing these features are not commonly exploited by academic librarians. Some libraries employ additional technologies, such as GAIM or Trillian, to allow librarians to combine multiple instant messaging services into one interface. Others use contact centre services, such as tutor.com, QuestionPoint and Docutek – these are more expensive, but are often run by a vendor who provides support for the technology. Contact centre services offer enhanced features, such as co-browsing, automatic statistics gathering and reporting, file-sharing and communication features such as pointers and highlighting that help librarians communicate with patrons. They may also offer staffing during extended hours. Numerous articles and presentations compare various contact centre services (Coffman, 2003; Houghton and Schmidt, 2005).

Instruction in the virtual reference environment

In the early 2000s many academic libraries began to offer a reference service via chat technology. At first librarians focused on the mechanics of the service, including deploying the technology, providing staffing and collecting statistics, and on methods for delivering accurate, fast reference services. Many librarians expected patrons to use virtual reference as they use the phone, mostly for ready-reference questions or troubleshooting and only rarely for questions that require instruction. Over time, librarians realised that a significant amount of virtual reference interaction can be described as one-on-one instruction. For example, Johnston (2003: 31) found that 60 per cent of the University of New Brunswick's virtual reference interactions had an instructional component. Desai and Graves (2006: 178) found that 83 per cent of virtual reference interactions at Southern Illinois University Carbondale featured instruction.

Instruction in the chat environment is similar to the one-to-one, point-of-need instruction that occurs at a physical reference desk. In both environments patrons initiate the reference transaction in real time at their time of need, when they are most open to learning (Beck and Turner, 2001: 83). In addition, instruction provided via in-person or virtual reference services is '"authentic" in that the student has a specific project underway and has specific questions regarding how to proceed' (Elmborg, 2002: 458). However, virtual reference offers a major advantage: students can get specific, individual instruction that is available regardless of location (Grassian and Kaplowitz , 2001: 195). On the other hand, instruction in the virtual reference environment offers two major challenges. First, the lack of physical proximity means that neither librarians nor patrons can use non-verbal communication. Second, many librarians and patrons speak much more quickly than they type, so the virtual reference encounter can be frustratingly slow.

Because of these challenges, librarians must learn techniques to facilitate instruction in the virtual reference environment.

Furthermore, because the challenges of the technology can occupy much of a librarian's thought during the interaction, librarians must actively focus on the instruction component of the interaction, and not allow impatience or distraction to cause them simply to answer and not to teach.

Suggestions for virtual reference instructors

The instructional role of virtual reference is a growing one. Librarians who provide virtual reference often encounter opportunities to fill gaps between what patrons know and what they must learn in order to complete a task. These 'teachable moments' offer librarians the chance to contribute to patrons' information literacy skill set. Suggestions for making the most of instructional opportunities in the virtual reference environment can be found in the library literature, at professional conferences and in conversations between providers of virtual reference. The following strategies describe ways in which librarians can reinforce patrons' metacognitive strategies for learning, encourage patrons' active engagement in the learning process and employ instructional techniques rooted in social constructivist learning theory. All of these techniques can improve the information literacy skill level of library users.

Strategies that encourage metacognition

Metacognition is often defined as 'thinking about thinking', or the ability to be intentional and reflective about one's thoughts. Expert thinkers and learners are metacognitively aware of their mental processes. When working to solve a problem, they remember methods that they have tried in the past, with both positive and negative results. They actively refine their problem-solving strategies based on what is empirically known, what others have experienced and what works best for them as individuals. Research indicates that people who employ metacognitive behaviours can more easily describe the initial state of a problem they want to solve, the goals they need to achieve to solve the problem, the tools they have at their disposal and any constraints or barriers barring the path to achieving the solution (Davidson and Sternberg, 1998: 50). Because metacognitive behaviour is the hallmark of an expert learner and thinker, reference librarians should seek to develop metacognitive skills in their patrons. Librarians should expect to encounter patrons with widely varying metacognitive abilities. By integrating the following strategies into their virtual reference service, librarians can reinforce the skills patrons currently have and model skills patrons still need to acquire.

Catch patrons being good

In virtual reference transactions, reference librarians should actively reinforce the positive information-seeking behaviours patrons demonstrate. Librarians who acknowledge and complement patrons' behaviours achieve three goals.

First, they reveal to users that information-seeking is not random, but rather is a logical problem-solving process. As a result, users feel reassured that they are taking steps to solve their information needs. They also become aware – or are reminded – that there are frameworks upon which information is structured. Patrons can apply new knowledge of information structures to solve their information needs.

Second, librarians who catch patrons being good provide positive reinforcement of skills. Patrons feel that the information expert recognises their hard work and that the information search they conducted before contacting a librarian was useful. Even patrons who have not engaged in preliminary information-seeking before contacting a librarian can be praised for their decision to seek expert assistance!

Third, providing positive reinforcement offers librarians a way to cement productive behaviours in the patrons' minds and minimise their mistakes. As a result, when patrons look back on the information-seeking experience they are more likely to recall the behaviours librarians wish them to add to their repertoire of information-seeking strategies.

Providing patrons with positive reinforcement requires an overt effort from librarians who are accustomed to providing fast service. While responsive service is important, it should be noted that positive reinforcement can be given quickly and produces valuable results.

Example 1
Librarian: I'm glad you can remember some of the words in the title.
Librarian: That will help us do a good search.
Librarian: Knowing the author's last name allows us to do a really thorough search.

Example 2
Librarian: That is a really good point.
Librarian: As you've said, you need to make sure you are using an authoritative website.
Librarian: Many people don't realise how important that is.
Librarian: Well done!

Example 3
Librarian: This is a great question!

Librarian: I can tell that you've already thought a lot about this topic.

Librarian: You already know what types of sources you need to answer the question, and you also know that you need to present both sides of the issue you're researching.

Librarian: That gives us a lot of information to start our search with.

Example 4

Librarian: I'm so glad you contacted us to assist you with this!

Librarian: Often, the best way to get this kind of specialised information is to ask an information professional.

Think aloud

In the virtual reference environment, librarians have opportunities to conduct personalised textual dialogue with patrons. In these dialogues, librarians should make the effort to make their thoughts, as expert searchers, transparent to patrons.

The 'think aloud' instructional technique employs three steps. First, the librarian internalises the patron's reference need and treats it as his/her own. Second, the librarian identifies the parts of the information-seeking process that the patron has already accomplished. (This step provides an opportunity to employ the 'catch them being good' strategy.) Third, the librarian describes his/her cognitive process throughout the remaining steps of the reference transaction. The third step of this process is the most difficult for many librarians, as the librarian must resist the temptation to take a mental 'short cut' to the patron's answer. However, making the effort to reveal internal thought processes allows librarians to achieve two important goals.

First, thinking aloud allows patrons insight into the expert information-seeking process of librarians. Patrons can learn how librarians define an information need, or what tools librarians use and why they used them. They can learn about how to evaluate the sources that are found and how to use them ethically. This strategy allows patrons a window into the minds of information professionals as they wrestle with the patrons' information needs. Patrons can seek clarification, ask questions and compare their own techniques with those the librarian suggests.

Second, by making the information-seeking process transparent to patrons, librarians can share not only their successful strategies but also the failures. In many cases, failed information-seeking strategies are even more instructive to patrons than successful ones. When a strategy fails, librarians are placed in situations patrons often encounter. However, librarians can reveal strategies for coping with failure by thinking aloud through why the strategy failed, what could be adjusted and when to try an entirely new technique. Patrons share in the journey and can benefit from witnessing the struggle.

Finally, because patrons often save the transcripts of virtual reference transactions, they can 'replay' their conversation with a librarian whenever they encounter similar information needs. Consequently, librarians should not hesitate to put energy and enthusiasm into their virtual reference transactions – their words may live on far longer than they think!

It is important to note that while the 'think aloud' strategy allows librarians to make their thought process visible to patrons, it should not be used to dominate the reference transaction conversation. Rather, this method should be employed sporadically throughout the dialogue, especially when patrons ask librarians to help them make decisions during the information-seeking process. Librarians will find this technique most useful if they maintain the role of 'guide' or 'facilitator'.

Example 1
Librarian: You're looking for a book that your teacher recommended, and you know that the title has the word 'wrinkle' in it and it's about time travel.
Librarian: Hmm...
Librarian: I think the best thing to recommend is a search in the NoveList database.
Librarian: That's a good database for doing a search when you know a 'keyword' from the title and something about the plot.
Librarian: How does that strategy sound to you?

Example 2
Librarian: OK, I see you're using the terms 'anti-smoking campaign'.
Librarian: I'll enter the same terms in the search box.
Librarian: Hmm... no results. Well, that happens sometimes.
Librarian: Let's try another way of saying that...
Librarian: How about 'smoking cessation'? Does that get at your topic, too?
Librarian: Great. That worked much better! Sometimes databases use different terms than those we use in conversation. It's always a good idea to be flexible and experiment with different words.

Show, do not tell

In virtual reference transactions, reference librarians often have the opportunity not only to describe the information-seeking process but also to demonstrate it. While the 'think aloud' technique highlights the importance of making expert information-seeking processes clear to novice library users, this strategy goes a step further. Whenever possible librarians should show, not tell, patrons the steps of the information-seeking process.

The options librarians have for showing patrons the information-seeking process vary depending on the technology used to provide the virtual reference service. This strategy may include 'co-browsing' webpages with patrons, 'pushing' prepared slides, audio files or tutorials to the patron or making an effort to direct patrons through opening a browser window and completing the steps during the chat. Regardless of method, it is important to move beyond narrative to images and interaction.

Librarians who use technology to engage patrons with visuals and real-time interactions achieve the important goal of addressing multiple learning styles. When librarians show, rather than tell, patrons how to proceed through the information-seeking process, they can appeal to their visual, auditory and kinesthetic learning modalities. By addressing more than one learning style, patrons are more likely to internalise and retain the lessons they learn during the virtual reference transaction.

Example
Librarian: OK, now that we know your keywords, let's get started with searching for the books you need.
Librarian: I'm going to begin pushing you pages. The first is the library homepage [www.library.org]. Do you see that?
Librarian: Super. Now... I'm going to click the link labelled 'Catalog' at the top of the screen [www.library. org/catalog].

Librarian: Go ahead and enter your keywords in the search box.

Librarian: Well done. I'll hit search for you [www.library.org/catalog/search].

Librarian: This is a nice result list! What looks good to you?

Take patrons to the next step

In virtual reference transactions, reference librarians should assist patrons with their immediate information needs and identify any additional steps the patron will face after the immediate need is met. Librarians may make patrons aware of coming challenges and opportunities, offer advice or, if patrons are ready to move to the next step, continue the reference transaction. During longer transactions patrons may need time to work independently to complete a step. In such cases, librarians can 'step out' of the conversation and re-enter when patrons are ready to continue. When patrons complete their information-seeking process, librarians should encourage them to return to the virtual reference service when a new need arises.

Librarians who guide patrons to the next step of the information-seeking process reinforce the concept that information-seeking is a logical process. Once patrons view information-seeking as a process that can be learned, they can employ metacognitive techniques and gain ownership of the process. Patrons who already have strong metacognitive skills in other domains can transfer what they know about their thinking and learning to the information environment. Whatever the information problem – undefined information needs, lack of familiarity with information tools, difficulty negotiating barriers to information – librarians can use reference transactions to explain the information environment to patrons, broaden their perspective beyond their immediate stage of the information-seeking process and assist with the transfer of skills from other domains to the library world. In short, by reinforcing metacognitive behaviour, librarians can help patrons become more information literate.

Example 1
Librarian: Great!
Librarian: Now that you've selected citations for several articles that interest you, the next step is to figure out how to put your hands on the full text of the articles.
Librarian: Are you ready to go to that step?

Example 2
Librarian: I'm so glad we were able to find some books that look promising for your project.
Librarian: Eventually, you'll need to cite your sources in order to give credit to the authors and explain where you found your information.
Librarian: We can talk more about that now or you can come back later.
Librarian: What sounds best to you?

Example 3
Librarian: Well, since you need ten sources of different types...
Librarian: Let's take it one source type at a time. This will be more efficient, since the paths for finding books and finding articles are pretty different.
Librarian: Let's start with finding some relevant articles...
Librarian: Books will come afterwards. Sound OK?

Librarian: Those terms worked great... this looks like a really good list of articles!

Librarian: If you click on the names of the articles, you can see the full text.

Librarian: Look through those and let me know when you've found what looks good...

Librarian: I'll be here when you're ready to make decisions or switch to searching for books.

Strategies that promote active learning

Active learning is a central tenet of constructivist learning theory and widely accepted as a cornerstone of effective instruction. When people actively participate in real-world activities and problem-solving, learning occurs. Librarians can use active learning techniques during virtual reference transactions to engage patrons in effective information-seeking behaviour.

Let patrons drive

Because users learn more quickly and thoroughly when they are actively engaged in the learning process, it is important to 'let them drive' during virtual reference transactions. Librarians who employ this strategy can begin transactions by inviting patrons to describe or show what steps they have already taken in their information-seeking process. Throughout the reference transaction, librarians can encourage patrons to initiate actions while the librarian observes. When virtual reference technology allows, librarians and patrons can work together in the same screen space to solve information problems. The overriding principle for this strategy is to allow patrons to make decisions and take actions while librarians serve as guides who can make connections, help patrons see patterns, ask relevant questions and encourage reflection.

Librarians who engage patrons in active learning achieve a number of goals. First, allowing patrons to drive provides librarians with the ability to view patrons' information-seeking behaviours and identify areas to improve or reinforce. The observation of patron behaviour not only helps librarians assist individuals, but may also contribute to librarians' understanding of the behaviour of entire user groups over time and the identification of barriers to information that were previously unknown. Second, the use of this technique has the added benefit of ensuring that patrons are actively participating in the reference transaction rather than passively waiting for problems to be solved for them. When virtual reference software allows shared screen space, patrons and librarians can achieve true collaboration and become partners in the information-seeking process.

Example 1
Librarian: I understand that you're having difficulties finding articles in this database on your topic.
Librarian: Why don't you redo the search in the space you see to the left of this text chat?
Librarian: Then I can see what happened and we can work together to fix it.

Example 2
Librarian: OK, so now you see that there are at least five websites that seem to answer your question.
Librarian: Why don't you click on each of your results, and we'll look at them together and talk about what might make one better than the others for your project.

Strategies that welcome patrons to the community of learners

According to social constructivist theory, what people learn is socially developed through interactions with 'expert' members of a specific community. By interacting with community members, novice learners are acculturated in the knowledge and skills of the group before joining a community of expert learners. According to Elmborg (2002: 458), librarians who adopt a social constructivist model of instruction can guide patrons to become members of a community of information-literate people. By adopting specific strategies, virtual reference librarians can acclimatise patrons to the information community.

Welcome patrons to the community

Virtual reference transactions offer an opportunity for librarians to support novice information-seekers as they progress towards membership in the community of expert information-seekers. To use this method successfully, librarians must focus on the goal: to prepare a new member to join their community. To achieve this goal, librarians should show enthusiasm for patron requests for assistance. They should also respond to patrons in the context of a community of learners by explaining that others wrestle with the same issues, fostering a climate of collaboration and recognising that patrons will pass on what they learn to others. Librarians should provide definitions for specialised community language, offer to confide 'tricks of the library trade' to patrons and explain the ethics, standards or history of library services and policies when relevant. Finally, librarians should actively elicit feedback from patrons as peers and the newest members of the information-literacy community.

Example 1

Librarian: I'm so glad you contacted us with this request!

Librarian: I see you found many web resources that are helpful.

Librarian: I can show you how we librarians pick and choose among them to find the best.

Librarian: Then you can show what you've learned to the other members of your team.

Example 2

Librarian: You're right... it's hard to know which database to select to search for an article on a specific topic of interest.

Librarian: One thing we at the library do is share among ourselves which ones have worked best for certain types of research.

Librarian: For your research, I'd recommend using the database listed first.

Librarian: I've had success with that in the past.

Librarian: Let's try it together.

Example 3

Librarian: Actually, that link takes you to the full text of electronic books that we don't have in print.

Librarian: I guess the name of the link is confusing, isn't it?

Librarian: What would you label it? I can pass your ideas on and maybe we can get it changed.

Librarian: The library website is constantly improving, due in large part to recommendations from patrons with good ideas!

Redirect to more social services when necessary

In virtual reference transactions, librarians should direct patrons to other reference venues or specialised librarians when appropriate. As a rule, virtual reference librarians should respond to patrons as completely as possible in the primary transaction. However, they may also wish to transfer the patron seamlessly to another form of reference communication if the patron's instructional needs can be better met by an alternative medium. Librarians may also make referrals to other library staff members who can augment the transaction with a specialised level of expertise. The referral might take the form of a second librarian entering the chat, a library staff member calling the patron with additional information or the provision of additional contact information to the patron so that a consultation can be scheduled.

The goal of a redirection in a virtual reference environment is to facilitate the acclimatisation of patrons into the community of information-literate people by providing instruction in the most efficient and effective manner. If the patron's needs are specialised, it may be that an expert librarian can offer additional information that will facilitate the acculturation process. Thus the goal of a referral to another library staff member is to ensure that the patron is brought into the proper community of specialisation.

Example 1
Librarian: It seems we have answered this question as well as we can in an instant messaging environment.
Librarian: If you want to share a screen with me, I can redirect you to http://library.org/askus and we can begin a different kind of chat that will allow us to see the same screen as we search for your resources.

Example 2
Librarian: This is the sort of troubleshooting that could be done more quickly by phone.
Librarian: Is there a phone number I can reach you at?
Librarian: If I call you, we can get past this hurdle

faster, and then I can show you how to cite these sources properly.

Example 3
Librarian: My colleague is an expert in this area.
Librarian: I'll get you started with this search, and then he will log on and give you some detailed advice about how to choose your sources.

Example 4
Librarian: You say you'll be coming to the library this week? That's great!
Librarian: Our Special Collections department has some unique artefacts you might find really relevant to your research.
Librarian: When you're here in person, you can take a look at these items.
Librarian: Be sure to talk with the Special Collections librarians – they can give you really good advice about how to work them into your project.

Focus on patron learning

Whatever techniques virtual reference librarians choose to employ, the guiding principle of instruction in the virtual reference environment is to keep the focus on the patrons and their learning. Using techniques that encourage metacognition, active learning and community-building is critical to the instructional quality of transactions. Librarians who expend effort using these instructional strategies need not focus on minor details of the virtual reference transaction.

- *Do not wordsmith.* In the virtual reference environment, patrons may feel disconnected if the librarian's presence is not evident. As a result, it is important that librarians keep the stream of words flowing. Instead of composing whole sentences and paragraphs and sending them in large chunks, librarians should send shorter segments and thoughts. The use of commas and ellipses signals to patrons that more information is coming.

Preferred

- Librarian: This is a great question! [8 seconds]
- Librarian: Let me think a second... [4 seconds]
- Librarian: Where should we look for this first... hmm... [6 seconds]
- Librarian: Well, if you're looking for scholarly sources, [8 seconds]
- Librarian: then that means we could begin with the catalog... [12 seconds]
- Librarian: or some article databases... [4 seconds]
- Librarian: or did you have another plan that you were thinking of? [9 seconds]

Not preferred

- Librarian: That's a great question. Because you said that you need a scholarly source, I think we should begin with the catalogue or maybe an article database that is general in nature but which has an option to limit for scholarly articles. Did you have any places that you thought we should look first or a database that you've already tried? [1 minute 15 seconds]

■ *Do not worry about speed.* While patrons increasingly value and expect instant gratification, it is important that librarians remember that not all virtual reference transactions require speedy 'ready-reference' responses. Indeed, many virtual reference questions require instructional responses. Once librarians determine that the goal of a specific transaction is to teach, they should employ strategies that facilitate learning, even when those strategies require a bit more time.

- *Do not focus on your grammar, spelling or capitalisation.* In order to focus on instructional strategies and maintaining visibility with patrons, sometimes grammar, spelling and capitalisation suffer. Unless the errors interfere with communication between librarians and patrons, they should be acceptable. Fixing such errors should not take high priority in virtual reference transactions.

Future directions for instruction in the virtual reference environment

As virtual reference technology evolves, the challenges addressed in this chapter may be eliminated. Technology that allows for fast and reliable voice and video should overcome the absence of non-verbal communication in virtual reference interactions. Ideally, new chat technology will offer increased functionality to support instruction, such as the ability to annotate webpages discovered during the interaction, highlight text for both the librarian and patron to see or handwrite on the screen as one does with a tablet PC or PDA.

In addition to technological advancements, assessment offers a path to future directions for instruction in the virtual reference environment. Because virtual reference technology generates a transcript of the interaction, assessment can be undertaken easily. Woodard (2005: 208) suggests that librarians review their transcripts with a peer coach to help improve service. Ellis (2004: 110) describes analysing transcripts for ACRL Information Literacy Competency Standards. Because transcripts can serve as evidence of student learning, they can be used to identify new virtual reference instruction techniques, determine their effectiveness and ensure a bright future for instruction in the virtual reference environment.

References

Beck, Susan E. and Turner, Nancy B. (2001) 'On the fly bi: reaching and teaching from the reference desk', *Reference Librarian*, 72: 83–96.

Coffman, Steve (2003) *Going Live: Starting & Running a Virtual Reference Service*. Chicago: American Library Association.

Davidson, Janet E. and Sternberg, Robert J. (1998) 'Smart problem solving: how metacognition helps', in Douglas J. Hacker, John Dunlosky and Arthur C. Graesser (eds) *Metacognition in Educational Theory and Practice*. Mahwah, NJ: Lawrence Erlbaum Associates, pp. 47–68.

Desai, Christina M. and Graves, Stephanie J. (2006) 'Instruction via instant messaging reference: what's happening?', *The Electronic Library*, 24(2): 174–89.

Ellis, Lisa A. (2004) 'Approaches to teaching through digital reference', *Reference Services Review*, 32(2): 103–19.

Elmborg, James K. (2002) 'Teaching at the desk: toward a reference pedagogy', *Portal: Libraries and the Academy*, 2(3): 455–64.

Grassian, Esther S. and Kaplowitz, Joan R. (2001) *Information Literacy Instruction*. New York: Neal-Schuman.

Houghton, Sarah and Schmidt, Aaron (2005) 'Web-based chat vs instant messaging: who wins?', *Online*, 29(4): 26–30.

Johnston, Patricia E. (2003) 'Digital reference as an instructional tool: just in time and just enough', *Searcher*, 11(3): 31–3.

Woodard, Beth S. (2005) 'One-to-one instruction: from the reference desk to online chat', *Reference & User Services Quarterly*, 44(3): 203–9.

4

Mobile computing
Joe M. Williams

For the purposes of this chapter, the phrase 'mobile computing' refers to those technologies or combinations of tools that enable computer access from almost any place at any time. Technologies that enable mobile computing, such as personal digital assistants (PDAs), tablet PCs, laptops, web-enabled cell phones and wireless networking options, have become more sophisticated and more commonplace in the last few years. As consumers take increasing advantage of these mobile technologies, their expectations for accessing remote content anywhere at any time increase as well. In response, libraries have begun considering mobile users when planning access services and physical space (Embrey, 2002: 24; Hiremath and Gudodagi, 2005; McCullough, 2003: 393; Wilson, 2004: 328).

For example, free wireless access and laptop services are now standard fare in many academic and public libraries. The new challenge for academic librarians is to identify and understand these rapidly evolving mobile technologies, and to find logical and useful ways to incorporate them into the delivery of instructional services. This chapter will highlight some of the most current, stable wireless networking options available today, and will discuss some different types of mobile devices and their present or potential applications to library instruction.

There are a number of reasons why academic librarians – and particularly instruction librarians – should pay close attention to mobile computing. First of all, the library patrons we serve are currently using and depending upon mobile tools for information access and management. Sales of PDAs, cellular phones and laptops have all risen consistently over the past few years and these technologies are beginning to appear in libraries with more frequency. The market for mobile devices is booming. Meanwhile, IT entrepreneurs and stalwart corporations are racing to develop the ultimate 'all-in-one' mobile device that combines telephony, high-speed wireless internet, and personal computing and multimedia functions.

Second, infrastructures that support mobile computing are becoming commonplace. Many municipalities, museums and higher education institutions have incorporated wireless networking into their infrastructure. Municipal business districts, such as downtown Portland, Houston, Philadelphia and Buffalo, now offer free or moderately priced internet access to any visitor with a wireless-enabled device. Many businesses, from privately owned coffeeshops to nationally franchised book retailers, now provide wireless connectivity to their patrons as part of their business plan.

Many colleges and universities have also begun supplementing their existing network infrastructures with wireless (Barnett-Ellis and Charnigo, 2005) and started integrating mobile computing into their curricula. Examples of curricular integration include the use of PDAs at North Carolina State University's College of Veterinary Medicine (www.cvm.ncsu.edu/mobilecomp/), the incorporation of tablet PCs at Virginia Institute of Technology's College of Engineering (Wu, 2006), Duke University's iPod initiative (www.duke.edu/ddi/projects/ipod.html) and Apple's growing iTunes-U programme (www.apple.com/education/products/ipod/itunes_u.html).

In addition to providing infrastructure, many academic institutions and businesses are also designing and providing their content with mobile users in mind. In general, website design trends now favour fast-loading, 'wireless-friendly' pages. Many news agencies and magazines now provide PDA- and Blackberry-compatible versions of their content, either delivered directly through the publisher's site or via a third-party provider such as AvantGo.com. Many instructors now make their lecture materials available to students online before, during or after class. Some instructors design their notes and slides to encourage student note-taking by laptop or tablet during lectures. The Blackboard Course Management System (www.blackboard.com/) is developing PDA integration of course content so that mobile users can view class announcements, calendar items, grades and course materials offline. Lastly, mobile computing offers libraries new opportunities for connecting with patrons and providing instruction, as described later in this chapter.

In short, there is a growing expectation of wireless availability and mobile content among today's library users. Information is being created for and delivered through these devices, so libraries would do well to understand these new media. To take a step further, it is proactive for libraries to adopt new mobile technologies and incorporate these new means of information delivery into their current delivery of educational materials. When providing these and other materials to mobile users, one technology often relied upon is some form of wireless connectivity.

Wireless networking

There are several types of wireless connectivity available today, with new standards constantly being developed and tested. The international non-profit organisation the IEEE (Institute of Electrical and Electronics Engineers) leads the creation and refinement of perhaps the best-known suite of wireless standards, the wireless local area network standards 802.11a, b and g.

The 802.11 wireless local area network (WLAN) or 'Wi-Fi' standards specify an '"over-the-air" interface between a wireless client and a base station or access point, as well as among wireless clients' (LAN/MAN Standards Committee, 1999). There are a number of amendments to the base 802.11 standard, each of which addresses particular aspects of the base standard such as security or connection speed. At the time of writing, the 802.11b and g standards are the typical wireless implementations that patrons generally install in their homes or encounter in places like libraries, coffeeshops and airports. Standard 802.11b, ratified in 1999, accommodates connection speeds of 11 Mbits (megabits) per second and the signal can be used up to approximately 330 feet from an access point. Standard 802.11g, ratified in 2004, accommodates much higher connection speeds (54 Mbits/sec) and can be used over shorter distances, approximately 100 feet from an access point.

With these Wi-Fi connections, the patron's mobile computing device – a wirelessly enabled laptop, tablet PC, PDA, etc. – establishes a wireless connection to the network via an access point located somewhere in the general vicinity. The access point is physically connected by cable to an underlying wired network, i.e. the library's LAN or an ISP connection.

The 802.11b standard relies on the Wired Equivalancy Protocol (WEP) for securing the data being passed wirelessly over the connection. During the past few years many security flaws have been discovered in the WEP. Therefore, many organisations offering 802.11b networks also require a virtual private network (VPN) connection for added security. VPN connections require that an additional piece of software – a VPN client – be present on the patron's mobile device. The VPN client is used to authenticate the user, and to establish a secure communication tunnel between the patron's device and the wireless access point. A more recent WLAN standard ratified in 2004 – 802.11i – addresses the WEP security issues and potential inconvenience of VPN use.

Beyond these Wi-Fi standards, there are other possibilities for sharing information wirelessly. Most PDAs and data-capable cell phones, as well as laptops and tablet PCs, now come equipped to share and receive data via infrared technology. Infrared connections cover a very short distance (approximately three feet) and are often used to transfer files between devices, such as transferring photos from a cell phone to a laptop. Infrared is also used with mobile computers to communicate with printers, audio headphones, keyboards and other peripheral devices.

Wireless personal area networks (WPANs) provide another alternative method of connecting and communicating. WPANs generally connect mobile devices to one another over short distances. One of the best-known current WPAN technologies is Bluetooth, which provides a secure connection between mobile devices and other mobile devices or peripherals for data-sharing. Like the Wi-Fi standards, the IEEE standards for WPANs – 802.15.1 – are constantly being developed and amended.

Mobile devices

Discussions of mobile technology often assume the presence of wireless networks and wirelessly connected devices. However, non-connected devices can also play an active role in library instructional services. One of the great benefits of mobile devices is their ability to provide information at the point of need. With adequate memory and storage capabilities, a mobile device does not need to be connected to the internet or network in order to provide this timely information. Many mobile computing initiatives rely on laptops, tablet PCs or PDAs used in an 'offline' or non-networked mode.

Loading instructional and reference materials on to a mobile device ensures that all students or patrons have the same timely information at their disposal. For instance, library patrons could access a pre-loaded tutorial on their laptop while in a study room, or consult a textbook or set of notes on their PDA during lectures. This 'quick reference' ability drives many clinical mobile computing initiatives today, as healthcare professionals and students access clinical resources from the bedside or examination room.

For the instructor, mobile computing can allow customisation of the classroom environments as situations demand. For example, a library instructor may want to hold a class in the stacks near relevant materials, or send students into the stacks with computers to work in specific areas of a collection or facility. The mobile environment allows for impromptu reorganisation and regrouping of students, with participants taking their computers and related files with them (see Chapter 5 for more on this topic).

PDAs and cell phones

Designing content for very small form factor devices, such as PDAs and data-enabled cell phones, presents several challenges to the content creator. The designer should keep in mind the following limitations of these devices.

- PDAs and cell phones have significantly smaller screen sizes and resolutions. The limitation of screen size requires the content designer to know the audience well, in order to understand what information patrons really want to access and use from their mobile devices. Taking time to understand the search habits and expectations of your small form factor users can help you design more effective content and interfaces.

- PDA and data phone users have different expectations to patrons accessing information from a traditional web browser. For instance, scrolling through pages of information on these very small devices is sometimes difficult and can become frustrating. Whenever possible, keep your content on one screen and offer a simple hyperlink or tab/button to navigate patrons to more content, rather than asking them to scroll.

- Not all PDAs and web-enabled phones are equipped to open and read a wide range of document formats. Devices running one of the two major PDA operating systems – Palm and Microsoft's Pocket PC – will usually have some sort of reader software that can open simple text files and basic html documents, but creating extensively formatted documents should be avoided. When offering files for download to a patron PDA or 'smart phone', consider also providing a link to compatible free reader software as well.

- Memory and processing speeds are often reduced compared to larger personal computers. If you are considering providing instructional materials for users to download to a PDA or data-enabled phone, the file sizes should be kept as small as possible with a minimum of low-resolution graphics.

There are a number of ways to incorporate PDAs and data-enabled phones into library instruction programmes. Some examples include the following.

- Create a kiosk or 'digital brochure rack' in the library containing instructional and/or frequently requested materials that patrons can beam on to their mobile devices (including laptops and tablet PCs) as needed.

- Create mechanisms for sending catalogue search results and other web-based instructional materials as a text message or SMS message to a patron's cell phone.

- Develop a PDA lending programme to help patrons explore the latest mobile technologies.

- Remember that PDAs are primarily personal information tools. So offering extended PDA checkouts for out-of-building use will allow borrowers to evaluate these devices fully by incorporating them into their daily personal routines.

- Take time to develop and load some instructional materials and 'help files' on to the PDAs you loan.

- PDAs are not especially complex devices to understand and use, but the user experience is significantly different from other mobile devices such as laptops. Allow ample time for staff training prior to lending the devices, and avoid mystifying the technology by designating one or more staff members as 'the PDA expert(s)'.

- Privacy issues can arise when patrons return borrowed PDAs with personal information in the memory or when patrons synchronise personal data on to a library PDA from a public terminal. Plan to remove personal data from all devices and terminals routinely.

- 802.11a, b and g wireless networks do not provide rigorous security. If patrons will be using library PDAs to send or receive personal information wirelessly, they should be notified of this risk at minimum. Ideally, a VPN client would be used to secure the wireless connections.

- Distribute PDAs during instructional sessions.

- Beam files to participants via infrared – class agenda, syllabi, lecture notes, etc.

- Have participants beam files to a partner – introductory information, answers to quiz questions during class, questions for the instructor.

- Ask participants to perform data entry tasks during the class, such as answering quiz or course evaluation questions. This requires developing data input forms in advance, and allotting class time for participants to beam their completed forms to the instructor.

Note that introducing PDAs into a classroom environment provides students with opportunities to cheat by sharing quiz answers with one another via infrared, or by looking up answers wirelessly on the internet. Also be mindful that, because of the discreet size and novelty of a PDA, students may be tempted to focus less on the class session and more on the technology. PDAs should be actively incorporated throughout a session in order to keep participants focused and engaged in the course content.

Laptops and tablet PCs

As with PDAs and data-enabled cell phones, laptops and tablet PCs can also be integrated into library instruction. Laptops and tablets have the added benefits of larger screen sizes, faster processing and easier screen navigation and data/text entry methods (mouse, touchpad and large keyboard). Tablet PCs have the added text entry feature of handwriting recognition/ink entry, where users write or draw with a stylus on the tablet screen as they would with a pen or brush on a sheet of paper. These mobile personal computers have the potential for increasing active learning in the classroom or other venue, enabling participants to explore and actively work through problems and concepts during class alone and in small groups.

Many libraries have developed laptop lending programmes for small group instruction sessions and/or patron checkout. Instructional materials can be pre-loaded on to these loaned computers in anticipation of user needs. Assessment tools can also be included on the desktop, enabling users to give feedback on specific classes, the lending programme or other library services.

For instruction, tablet PCs are particularly useful tools because of their handwriting functionality. This ink entry feature allows the instructor to annotate slides during lectures, or create handwritten slides as the class progresses. Participants with tablets in hand can annotate their copies of slides and lecture notes as well.

As mentioned earlier in this chapter, most newer laptops and tablets now come equipped with infrared ports, and some with Bluetooth capability. These wireless technologies allow for file-sharing among participants. Collaborative software, such as Tidebreak's TeamSpot, enables groups of laptop or tablet users to share a single display, similar to the co-browsing functionality of some virtual reference products. These collaborative applications often allow an instructor to 'give' the focus of the overhead display to different participants. So students can show each other their files or their search strategies and results in real time on a large classroom display.

Mobile computing devices are commonplace now, and the library patrons we serve are currently using and depending upon mobile tools for their information access and management. There is a growing expectation for wireless availability and mobile content among today's library users, and many libraries have begun considering mobile users when planning access services and physical spaces. As mobile technologies mature, the opportunities for incorporating these tools into library instruction services and programmes continue to grow as well.

References

Barnett-Ellis, P. and Charnigo, L. (2005) 'Wireless networks in medium-sized academic libraries: a national survey', *Information Technology and Libraries*, 24(1): 13–21.

Embrey, T.R. (2002) 'Library applications in support of the needs of students and teachers', *Teacher Librarian*, 29(5): 24–7.

Hiremath, Rahul R. and Gudodagi, Shashikant C. (2005) 'Anywhere anytime access to library: wireless application protocol (WAP)', *SRELS Journal of Information Management*, 42(1): 51–6.

LAN/MAN Standards Committee (1999) *IEEE Std 802.11b-1999 (R2003), Supplement to ANSI/IEEE Std 802.11.* IEEE Computer Society; available at: *http://standards.ieee.org/wireless/* (accessed: 27 October 2005).

McCullough, J. (2003) 'Redesigning library applications for PDAs: ILS vendor perspective', *Library Hi-Tech*, 21(4): 393–9.

Wilson, Paula (2004) 'Library service without wires: connectivity and content', *Public Libraries*, 43(6): 328–9.

Wu, Corinna (2006) 'Take a tablet', *ASEE Prism*, 16(4); available at: *www.eng.vt.edu/pdf/upload_files/ASEE%20PRISM%20-%20DECEMBER%202006.pdf* (accessed: 2 January 2007).

Further reading

Barak, Miri, Lipson, Alberta and Lerman, Steven (2006) 'Wireless laptops as means for promoting active learning in large lecture halls', *Journal of Research on Technology in Education*, 38(3): 245–63.

Bluetooth SIG (2006) 'Bluetooth technology: Learn'; available at: *www.bluetooth.com/Bluetooth/Learn/* (accessed: 27 December 2006).

Breeding, M. (2002) 'A hard look at wireless networks', *Library Journal*, Net Connect Supplement (Summer); available at: *www.libraryjournal.com/article/CA232340. html* (accessed: 27 December 2006).

Clyde, Laurel A. (2004) 'M-learning', *Teacher Librarian*, 32(1): 44–6.

Drew, William Jr (2002) 'The wireless student and the library', *Library Journal*, Net Connect Supplement (Summer); available at: *www.libraryjournal.com/article/ CA232339.html* (accessed: 27 December 2006).

Drew, William Jr (2003) 'Wireless networks: new meaning to ubiquitous computing', *Journal of Academic Librarianship*, 29(2): 102–6.

EDUCAUSE Learning Initiative and New Media Consortium (2007) *2007 Horizon Report*; available at: *www.educause.edu/ELIResources/10220* (accessed: 2 January 2007).

Graham, Rebecca A. (2002) 'Wireless use in libraries', *Library Hi-Tech*, 20(2): 237–40.

Le Ber, Jeanne Marie, Lombardo, Nancy T., Weber, Alice and Bramble, John (2004) 'Portable classroom leads to partnership', *Medical Reference Services Quarterly*, 23(2): 41–8.

Matesic, Maura (2003) 'Education, PDAs, and wireless networks: a new convergence', *College & Undergraduate Libraries*, 10(2): 19–28.

Providenti, Michael (2005) 'The art of the accessibility statement', *Internet Reference Services Quarterly*, 10(1): 7–62.

Rawlinson, David R. and Bartel, Kimberlee (2006) 'Implementing wireless PDA technology in the IT curriculum', *EDUCAUSE Quarterly*, 1: 41–7.

Rios, Gabriel R. (2004) 'PDA librarian', *Reference Services Review*, 32(1): 16–20.

Siff, Frederick H. (2006) 'Mobility and higher education: not just the next big thing', *ECAR Research Bulletin*, 22: 1–10.

5

Beyond the keyboard: optimising technology spaces for collaborative learning, instruction and service

Jennifer Sharkey

Introduction

Utilisation of technology in the classroom is becoming more and more diverse as the classroom environment changes to accommodate collaborative and active learning and faculty become more open to using new types of tools and applications. What about the computer and public-access workstations? Are they doomed to stay as static and stiff mono-stations or can they be modified and changed to promote collaborative instruction among multiple user groups, to enhance an active learning environment and to encourage unique delivery of services? It can be easily said that advances in technology and access to information have been the impetus for modifications to the traditional library.

Increasingly, universities are examining current classrooms and computer labs and implementing new types of learning spaces, which have given way to technology spaces that are mobile and modifiable to suit whatever type of learning and instruction is occurring within the space. For libraries, effective delivery of services and providing quality instruction are shaping how administrators, librarians and even patrons are envisioning library space.

As future technology becomes integrated into teaching and learning, academic librarians need to create spaces that accommodate the actual technology as well as how students use it. One needs to ask 'Is developing technology spaces based solely on student use and library services enough?' To create a space that is truly collaborative, one must examine student learning behaviour and faculty teaching patterns (Bennett, 2003). Various design models, both instructional and spatial, are being adopted for the next generation of library classrooms and learning spaces.

Historical significance of technology and the academic library

As computers became mainstream entities within the academic environment and the internet became a standard in finding and accessing information, it was not long before libraries began to institute instructional spaces that included computer labs. Instructional programmes began changing to accommodate online searching skills and introductions to multiple search interfaces.

During the late 1960s and into the 1970s the National Science Foundation (NSF) led the discussion about computer use and the computer science curriculum at the college level (Childers, 2003). As the NSF and professors discussed computers in academe, librarians were having a parallel discussion about library instruction and integration into the university curriculum (Lorenzen, 2001). During the early 1980s the public adopted the computer as a mainstream entity. Academic institutions were also implementing them, which included computers in libraries (Childers, 2003). The introduction of computer-based technologies, such as CD-ROMs and online catalogues and databases, soon affected and influenced instructional initiatives (Salony, 1995). Today, inclusion of information creation and retrieval technology tools is an expectation rather than a new or unique initiative. Electronic-based information sources influence the way we teach and deliver complementary services.

As new generations of technology emerge, instruction has moved from accessing electronic sources to capturing, manipulating and creating information – thus leading the profession to examine library spaces as a way to promote learning and influence how services are delivered.

Emergence of the information commons

Scenario
Susan's group is planning on meeting at the library to finalise their presentation. She would have preferred to meet somewhere else, even though some of the resources they need are at the library and they can get help from the librarian. The computers by the reference desk do not have the presentation application they need to use. The library computer lab, which has the needed application, does not allow more than one student to sit at a computer. One of the other team members has a laptop but even if she remembers to bring it, group study rooms and power outlets are in short supply.

The phrase 'information commons' started to emerge around the early 1990s. Beagle (1999) identifies two models in which this phrase is applied. One describes a library that focuses exclusively on online resources and access points. The other describes a physical space that provides equipment and services which allow students to find, access, manipulate and create information. It is this second model that has become synonymous with the phrase information commons. Today, the literature is filled with examples of information commons that have been built over the last 15 years. A common thread among many of these new library environments is the renovation or building of the physical space and the blending of IT and library services.

Bailey and Tierney (2002) examine the current state of information commons and build upon Beagle's model. They present three types of information commons: the world of information or the 'macro-commons'; areas of just computers and related technology or the 'micro-commons'; and the 'integrated commons' which focuses on learning, research and teaching. Additionally, they state that 'the central purpose of the... Information Commons is to provide informational services that facilitate and enhance the teaching-learning-research enterprise... both as it exists and as it develops a more substantive research character' (Bailey and Tierney, 2002: 284). The impact of utilising the information commons model is significant in that it typically becomes a blending of units, personnel and policy that were once distinct and separate from each other (Beagle, 1999).

As the multitasking millennials become the major users of the academic library, expectations to have access to the technology they use for research increase (Gardner and Eng, 2005). Today, more then ever, student projects are incorporating multiple types of software and hardware; providing this in the library where they conduct research is an important incorporation. By doing this students are no longer forced to move from facility to facility (MacWhinnie,

2003). Incorporating an information commons shifts how services, including instruction, are provided. Most importantly, it often changes the purpose and mission of the library. Should this focus move to a technology support structure or instruction? Beagle (2002: 290) holds that 'If instruction represents the single most important paradigm for libraries in the future, then the IC may yet become recognized as a laboratory for researching, prototyping, and assessing technological and pedagogical modalities.' Providing appropriate space for all types of learning as well as the 'laboratory' is notably one of the biggest challenges.

Creating spaces to enhance learning and teaching

Scenario

Jack and his friends in the learning community have the same class schedule on Mondays, Wednesdays and Fridays. The two-hour break he and his classmates have between classes is an ideal time to work on their group project for their information and society class. When working together as a group they typically need a whiteboard, a projector, a computer, a scanner, a large workspace, access to print advertisements in magazines and newspapers and occasionally conference time with their professor. Even though the class meets in the library, they rarely stay there to conduct group meetings. The library classroom would be an ideal space but students are not allowed to use it outside of a scheduled class.

In 2003 Scott Bennett wrote a report for the Council on Library and Information Resources that challenged the notion of creating library space around services and computer equipment. He urges planners to focus on learning behaviours and teaching instead. Ideally, a library has 'spaces where learning is the primary activity and where the focus is on facilitating the social exchanges through which information is transformed into the knowledge of some person or group of persons' (Bennett, 2003: 4). What constitutes an effective learning environment is dependent on a variety of factors. It is important to remember that 'learning is fundamentally a social construct that allows access to instruction, collaboration, informed research, relevant resources, critical analysis, and integrated results' (Wedge and Kearns, 2005: 32).

With great emphasis on the learning process and quality learning spaces, newly constructed or renovated spaces are now being labelled as learning commons. Is there really a difference between an information commons and a learning commons? Bennett draws a clear distinction between the two; specifically, 'information commons emphasize the interdisciplinary character of information and the power of digital technology' (Bennett, 2003: 37), while 'the core activity of a learning commons... [is] the collaborative learning by which students turn information into knowledge and sometimes into wisdom' (Bennett, 2003: 38). What is the vision of a new learning space? While no concrete formula exists, there are several approaches that can be utilised to ensure optimal use of the space.

The challenge for most facilities is working within the traditional square or rectangle layout of buildings and classrooms. Even though these structures will not change in the near future, advances in technology allow for alternate configurations. Moving away from the 'rectilinear configuration' (Forrest and Hinchliffe, 2005: 297) typically found in libraries to more mobile and wireless computing and gathering spaces creates an environment that encourages interaction and collaboration. Flexible space is essential to encourage and maintain collaboration among students and librarians, create relevancy within the university environment and accommodate a variety of learning behaviours and styles (Crockett et al., 2002; Forrest and Hinchliffe, 2005; McKinstry, 2004; Smith, 2004; Hurt, 1997).

Wedge and Kearns (2005: 38) highlight various types of flexibility.

- *Programming flexibility.* Designing space to support a variety of similar programme uses without any reconfiguration from use to use.

- *Spatial flexibility.* The ability of a space to be easily transformed to support a variety of different programme uses.

- *Structural flexibility.* The ability of a modular building structure to support a major reconfiguration of space over time, including the use of non-bearing walls and other quasi-permanent design elements.

- *Future expansion flexibility.* Designing space to accommodate long-term growth and change, including future building expansion, while developing or complying with a master plan.

Each of these types of flexibility provides a broad structure in which a new construction or renovation project can be developed. Forrest and Hinchliffe (2005: 299) present key elements a library can implement to establish flexible learning spaces.

- Small group gathering spaces for informal collaborative learning, with comfortable seating, adequate workspace and equipment and appropriate noise abatement.

- Computer clusters for more formal small group instruction using broadcast software (instead of projection) to send the instructor monitor image to the learning workstation monitors.

- Hands-on classrooms in both traditional rows and more flexible arrangements made possible by moveable furniture, laptops and wireless networking.

- Availability of classroom-on-wheels units with laptops and broadcast software to bring technology into learning spaces without permanent technology.

- Media viewing spaces with appropriate equipment.

- Event space for hosting guest lectures and discussions.

Lippencott (2004: 155) supports the idea of flexible technology spaces and says they 'need to have the capacity for relatively easy reconfiguration as needs will change over time'. Demas (2005: 31) introduces the idea of flexible 'minilabs' or a library that contains 'a rich suite of productivity processing tools and act as a Kinko's-like service center that enables students to find, manipulate, and create information'.

In addition to flexibility, a twenty-first-century learning space needs to be 'future-proofed, bold, creative, supportive, and enterprising' (JISC, 2006: 3). Since technology and furniture are on shorter replacement cycles, discussions need to include how the space can accommodate continual change (Johnson and Lomas, 2005). Valenti (2005: 40) recommends that an institution create a design team which should develop a 'design precept' that will 'describe the overall environment in which the learning space is being developed and help suggest the context in which the design team will formulate the project'. It is not uncommon for a redesign project to get embroiled in carpet swatches and paint chips. Having a master plan or precept can help maintain focus on the ultimate outcome – a space that supports the learning process and a variety of learning behaviours (Brown, 2005).

How a space is designed is greatly dependent on the individual institution and its learning vision and mission (Brown, 2005). However, the space design influences how individuals interact and communicate. For informal interactions 'niches' can be created. These are 'spaces where spontaneous interaction can occur and be maintained for at least a short time-frame, with the ability to establish eye contact, and a surface on which to work (e.g., jot down ideas, trade information)' (Scott-Weber, 2004: 71). Supporting this type of learning encourages and accommodates Generation Y's preference for casual yet collaborative learning. Informal learning within a library is a natural occurrence; however, formalised learning and teaching are just as important within learning spaces.

Impact on library instruction

Scenario
Tomaki rushes into class and quickly takes a seat, happy that he is not late. As a fourth-year international student, he needs this one-credit class to maintain his student visa and hopes it is not too boring. Jill, a first-year student on the university's swimming team, is taking the class to fill up her credit load. She hopes the class will not be too hard so she can maintain her GPA.

Instruction within a library takes many forms, such as online chat, one-to-one consultations, formal classroom instruction and even casual conversation. Who is teaching and who is learning shifts as the need arises, and in many cases it is not just librarian to student but often student to student. The very nature of teaching and learning continues to shift as transformations in both physical and virtual library spaces occur. The way information is found and created has moved the learning environment 'away from the simple transmission of information to an active acquisition of skills and knowledge' (Johnson and Lomas, 2005: 22). To meet the changing expectations and demands of users, old services are modified and refocused while new services are implemented. With new generations of technology, like iPods, wikis and blogs, structured library instruction can move in a new direction to support students already actively using the library and also to encourage more reluctant users.

The 2006 *Horizon Report* states that 'information literacy should not be considered a given even among "net-gen" students' (New Media Consortium, 2006: 4). Regular discussions within the library literature about information-literacy initiatives show academic librarians wholeheartedly agree that students today still need help attaining information-literacy skills. With large amounts of information readily accessible in the online environment, students can opt to use and find information that is quick to locate and download but not necessarily the best or most relevant. Librarians' involvement in student learning is more important now then ever before (MacWhinnie, 2003). The way learning spaces are designed as well how students are taught affects students' ability to learn and engage. However, a state-of-the-art facility alone does not ensure students automatically develop information-literacy or technology skills.

For many academic libraries, stand-alone credit courses offer students the opportunity to learn information-literacy skills at a deeper level than traditional guest lectures are able to provide. For any library credit class not integrated into the university's curriculum, teaching unmotivated students is a commonality and typically a regular discussion thread at conferences and in listservs. The manner in which assignments and class activities are developed and used within the classroom influences students' motivation (Jacobson and Xu, 2004). Technology can offer many alternatives in the teaching and learning environment which can help turn the unmotivated student into an interested and active participant.

Much of today's learning theory evolves around constructivism, which supports active and problem-based learning. Instruction developed using constructivist learning theory puts the focus of learning on:

- contextual – taking into account the student's understanding;

- active – engaging students in learning activities that use analysis, debate and criticism (as opposed to simply memorisation) to receive and test information;

- social – using discussions, direct interaction with experts and peers and team-based projects (Brown, 2005: 12.5).

Technology applied to these types of learning can facilitate communication, encourage critical thinking, support the discovery process and build community (Woodard, 2003). Using this broad picture of the learning environment it then becomes easy to identify potential technologies that could be integrated into curricula. The nature of social networking technologies alone caters to these elements quite well.

Just using technology within the classroom does not ensure successful implementation (Bates and Poole, 2003). Drawing from an experience with an integrated technology and information literacy course, Adalian et al. (1997: 21) note that 'students did not see the relationship between finding, evaluating, and presenting information'. The challenge then for librarians becomes identifying instructional methods and models that support good integration of both concepts. While some argue the drawbacks of using technology pre-empt its use in the classroom, many faculty and librarians see its value. Bates and Poole (2003: 51) clarify that 'the question then is not are they better or worse, but in what contexts and for what purposes are technologies best used?'. Identifying the context and purpose for technology falls to the planning and development of a course or curriculum. Most importantly, creating quality goals and learning outcomes establishes a foundation that ensures successful integration.

Most instructional design models support the development of learning objectives and outcomes; often a major step in the overall process. However, very few models focus specifically on technology integration. The information fluency model provides a big-picture approach for developing blended instruction. The model supports not only the integration of computing and information literacy skills, but also integrating critical thinking (ACS, 2003). Keeping this overall goal in mind, an instructor can then create broad learning outcomes which support these three skill sets.

An example of these types of outcomes can be seen in Purdue University Libraries information-literacy class, GS 175 Information Strategies. The learning outcomes are stated as being able to:

- differentiate between types of information;
- write a thesis statement for a project;
- find a variety of sources related to a selected topic;
- determine the relevance of a found source;
- create a documentary-style short film (Sharkey, 2005).

For those looking for more structure, the eTIPS (Educational Technology Integration and Implementation Principles) model comprises six principles that guide teachers and institutions with technology integration into curricula. While originally created to help K-12 teachers and schools meet state educational standards, three of the principles are easily applied to any instructional initiative:

- learning outcomes drive the selection of technology (eTIP 1);

- technology use provides added value to teaching and learning (eTIP 2);

- technology assists in the assessment of the learning outcomes (eTIP 3) (Dexter, 2002: 58–61).

To guide this model's application, use the following set of questions with each principle.

- eTIP 1: Which objectives or standards does the technology complement and support? Are these mainly content area objectives or process skills? What is the cognitive demand on learners as they use the technology?

- eTIP 2: How does using the technology add to what the teacher or students can do? Compared to other resources, what added value does the technology bring to the teacher or students' work? How does the time required for the integration of the technology balance with the instructional goals and objectives? Would using the technology require the teacher to overcome inordinately difficult logistics (i.e. to secure sufficient electrical outlets, tables or chairs and space...)?

- eTIP 3: What criteria will be used to evaluate student work? In the assessment, will the students' capability with the technology also be assessed? How can the students' technology-supported performance demonstrate progress toward specific objectives or standards? (Dexter, 2002: 66–7)

Asking these key questions ensures the appropriate technology is being used for the purpose of the course or project. When examining the types of information technologies used or implemented in learning spaces and within curricula, it is beneficial to look at their functionality. Most information technology integrated into learning spaces is distinctively grouped to fit four types of learning: mobile learning (laptops, PDAs), connected learning (wired and wireless networks), visual and interactive learning (smartboards, e-instruction) and supported learning (touch-screen kiosks, text-to-voice readers) (JISC, 2006: 6–7).

Combining these three elements of functionality, learning outcomes and added value creates the foundation on which successful integration can be built.

One challenge for many professors and librarians is establishing relevance between technology, the learner and projects or activities. Being aware of student characteristics and learning needs is an important part of instructional design. Visually linking characteristics or needs to various types of technologies or activities helps with curriculum development. Malcolm Brown (2005) breaks down a series of characteristics for Generation Y and identifies how these characteristics link to constructivist learning theory principles, as well as applying to information technology and learning spaces (Table 5.1).

Another challenge to implementing a new library concept is that of service. As users come to expect a seamless service environment, separate helpdesks are no longer adequate (Beagle, 1999; Crockett et al., 2002; McKinstry, 2004).

Table 5.1 Aligning net-gen characteristics, learning principles, learning space and IT applications

Net-gen trait	Learning theory principles	Learning space application	IT application
Group activity	Collaborative, cooperative, supportive	Small group work spaces	IM chat; virtual whiteboards; screen sharing
Goal and achievement orientation	Metacognition; formative assessment	Access to tutors, consultants and faculty in the learning space	Online formative quizzes; e-portfolios
Multitasking	Active	Table space for a variety of tools	Wireless
Experimental; trial and error	Multiple learning paths	Integrated lab facilities	Applications for analysis and research
Heavy reliance on network access	Multiple learning resources	IT highly integrated into all aspects of learning spaces	IT infrastructure that fully supports learning space functions
Pragmatic and inductive	Encourage discovery	Availability of labs, equipment and access to primary resources	Availability of analysis and presentation applications
Ethnically diverse	Engagement of preconceptions	Accessible facilities	Accessible online resources
Visual	Environmental factors; importance of culture and group aspects of learners	Shared screen (either projector or LCD); availability of printing	Image databases; media editing programs
Interactive	Compelling and challenging material	Workgroup facilitation; access to experts	Variety of resources; no 'one size fits all'

Today, campus departments blend to provide a variety of services and collaborative environments. However, creating boundaries which mark both space and duties typically defeats the true spirit of a learning environment (Lippincott, 2004). While integration of services may create tension among staff, key strategies to minimise these are staff training, continual communication and flexibility (Beagle, 2002; Crockett et al., 2002; McKinstry, 2004). As with learning space redesign, how services are planned and implemented is dependent on the individual institution.

With three distinct types of services typically found within a library or learning commons, the way they are implemented can determine success or failure of a space. One impact on the level of use is the location of a service desk as well as user work areas. Additionally, the types of staff available at service points and their level of training have immediate impact on users' confidence and desire to return for help. Lastly, the hours a facility is open dictate the number of students using it and even their ability to take advantage of the area (Mitchell, 2005). While current discussion gravitates toward the opinion that learning spaces should not be designed around services, users still expect to have common services such as reference. The format and method of delivery of services should be influenced by the users' needs and traits (Lippincott, 2006).

Conclusion

Scenario
Monique, Abdulla, Tomaki and Beth have been friends since freshman year, where they met in their learning community. Their twentieth-century American history course is the last class they will be taking together.

While challenging, it has been one of the best courses they have taken. They never thought history could be so much fun to learn. During class their professor uses movie clips, videoconferencing and group activities while they learn about events such as prohibition, the world wars, the civil rights movement and various presidential elections. Besides the historical events, the students also learn how to find different types of information sources such as historical newspapers, books, scholarly journals, websites and multimedia. The librarian liaison stays connected with them by posting information to the class blog, preparing activities they do in class and coming to give guest lectures. That helps immensely for the milestone assignment, where each group develops a critical analysis of information sources they plan to use to support the premise of the final project. This project is one of the highlights of the course and tonight the group will finish it. It requires them to create a digital film focused on a historical event they are learning about in class. Some of the groups are creating dramatic films but Monique's group chose to do a documentary. The class is taught in the newly built Magnum Learning Sphere and Monique's group meets there regularly after class to work on the various milestone assignments and the final project. Since it opened, the Sphere has been a big hit with the students. Designed with natural lighting, live plants and multiple learning zones, students can do everything from individual quiet study to casually hanging out or group collaboration while having the ability to access both print and electronic resources and do multimedia development. Open 24/7, the Sphere provides everything Monique's group needs for the project: a café for coffee and food, collaboration pods, digital equipment and multiple types of information sources. Each pod provides a high-end computer, a scanner, audio recording equipment, a webcam, a projector and a smartboard. The firewire-enabled computer is equipped with applications for a variety of development needs and accesses the university's virtual community and library. There are several digital development kits available to use in the Sphere or to check out. Monique's group checked out the film-making kits regularly for the documentary. About 20 feet away from the pods is a helpdesk, so when they run into trouble there is someone always available. The librarian liaison is often online for IM and chat sessions when they need expert help. When Monique started at the university three years ago, working on a project like this was possible but difficult since access to needed equipment and support was segregated or nonexistent.

No one really knows for sure what the library of the future will look like or encompass. The evolution of library space and services is moving from highly divided and delineated to integrated and complementary; modification of these spaces and services is now in progress. Library space, viewed as an environment to support multiple types of learning and teaching, is having the greatest transformation and influencing the delivery of services, including instruction.

The impact of technology both enhances and challenges faculty and librarians' ability to accommodate new generations of students and their learning preferences. The impact extends to all aspects of the academic library by changing the way information is accessed, how users receive support and the availability of tools for teaching and collaboration. Libraries that stay focused on learning as well as flexibile to accommodate change have the greatest chance of creating a space used and accepted by all members of its community.

References

ACS (2003) *ACS Information Fluency – Definition.* Atlanta: Associated Colleges of the South; available at: *www.colleges.org/~if/if_definition.html* (accessed: 29 September 2004).

Adalian, Paul T. Jr, Hoffman, Irene M., Rockman, Ilene F. and Swanson, Judy (1997) 'The student-centered electronic teaching library: a new model for learning', *Reference Services Review*, 25(3/4): 11–22.

Bailey, Russell and Tierney, Barbara (2002) 'Information commons redux: concept, evolution, and transcending the tragedy of the commons', *Journal of Academic Librarianship*, 28(5): 277–86.

Bates, A.W. and Poole, Gary (2003) *Effective Teaching with Technology in Higher Education: Foundations of Success*, Jossey-Bass Higher and Adult Education Series. San Francisco: Jossey-Bass.

Beagle, Donald (1999) 'Conceptualizing an information commons', *Journal of Academic Librarianship*, 25(2): 82–9.

Beagle, Donald (2002) 'Extending the information commons: from instructional testbed to Internet2', *Journal of Academic Librarianship*, 28(5): 287–96.

Bennett, Scott (2003) *Libraries Designed for Learning*, Vol. 122. Washington, DC: Council on Library and Information Resources; available at: *www.clir.org/pubs/reports/pub122/pub122web.pdf* (accessed: 30 November 2005).

Brown, Malcolm (2005) 'Learning spaces', in Diana G. Oblinger and James L. Oblinger (eds) *Educating the Net Generation*. EDUCAUSE, pp. 12.1–22; available at: *www.educause.edu/educatingthenetgen/* (accessed: 22 February 2006).

Childers, S. (2003) 'Computer literacy: necessity or buzzword?', *Information Technology and Libraries*, 22(3): 100–4.

Crockett, Charlotte, McDaniel, Sarah and Remy, Melanie (2002) 'Integrating services in the information common: toward a holistic library and computing environment', *Library Administration & Management*, 16(4): 181–6.

Demas, Sam (2005) 'From the ashes of Alexandria: what's happening in the college library?', in Geoffrey T. Freeman (ed.) *Library as Place: Rethinking Roles, Rethinking Space*, Vol. 129. Washington, DC: Council on Library and Information Resources; available at: *www.clir.org/pubs/reports/pub129/pub129.pdf* (accessed: 30 November 2005).

Dexter, Sara (2002) 'ETIPS – Educational Technology Integration and Implementation Principles', in Patricia L. Rogers (ed.) *Designing Instruction for Technology-Enhanced Learning*. Hershey, PA: Idea Group Publishing, pp. 56–70.

Forrest, Charles and Hinchliffe, Lisa Janicke (2005) 'Beyond classroom construction and design: formulating a vision for learning spaces in libraries', *Reference & User Services Quarterly*, 44(4): 296–300.

Gardner, Susan and Eng, Susanna (2005) 'What students want: Generation Y and the changing function of the academic library', *Portal: Libraries and the Academy*, 5(3): 405.

Hurt, C. (1997) 'Building libraries in the virtual age', *College & Research Libraries News*, February: 75–6, 91.

Jacobson, Trudi E. and Xu, Lijuan (2004) *Motivating Students in Information Literacy Classes*, New Library Series. New York: Neal-Schuman.

JISC (2006) *Designing Spaces for Effective Learning: A Guide to 21st Century Learning Space Design*; available at: *www.jisc.ac.uk/uploaded_documents/JISClearningspaces.pdf* (accessed: 21 May 2006).

Johnson, Chris and Lomas, Cyprien (2005) 'Design of the learning space: learning and design principles', *EDUCAUSE Review*, July/August: 16–28.

Lippincott, Joan K. (2004) 'New library facilities: opportunities for collaboration', *Resource Sharing and Information Networks*, 17(1/2): 147–57.

Lippincott, Joan K. (2005) 'Net generation students and libraries', in Diana G. Oblinger and James L. Oblinger (eds) *Educating the Net Generation*. EDUCAUSE, pp. 13.1–16; available at: *www.educause.edu/educating thenetgen/* (accessed: 22 February 2006).

Lorenzen, M. (2001) 'A brief history of library information in the United States of America (history of bi)', *Illinois Libraries*, 83(2): 8–18.

MacWhinnie, Laurie A. (2003) 'The information commons: the academic library of the future', *Portal: Libraries and the Academy*, 3(2): 241–57.

McKinstry, Jill (2004) 'Collaborating to create the right space for the right time', *Resource Sharing and Information Networks*, 17(1/2): 137–46.

Mitchell, Gregory A. (2005) 'Distinctive expertise: multimedia, the library, and the term paper of the future', *Information Technology and Libraries*, 24(1): 32–6.

New Media Consortium (2006) *The Horizon Report*. Austin, TX: New Media Consortium; available at: *www.nmc.org/pdf/2006_Horizon_Report.pdf* (accessed: 20 March 2006).

Salony, Mary F. (1995) 'The history of bibliographic instruction: changing trends from books to the electronic world', *The Reference Librarian*, 51/52: 31–51.

Scott-Weber, Lennie (2004) *In Sync: Environmental Behavior Research and the Design of Learning Spaces.* Ann Arbor, MI: Society for College and University Planning.

Sharkey, Jennifer (2005) *GS 175 Information Strategies.* Purdue University Libraries; available at: *http://web.ics. purdue.edu/~sharkeyj/gs175/* (accessed: 10 May 2005).

Smith, Stefan A. (2004) 'Designing collaborative learning experiences for library computer classrooms', *College & Undergraduate Libraries*, 11(2): 65–83.

Valentini, Mark S. (2005) 'Learning space design precepts and assumptions', *EDUCAUSE Review*, July/August: 40.

Wedge, Carole C. and Kearns, Thomas D. (2005) 'Creation of the learning space: catalysts for envisioning and navigating the design process', *EDUCAUSE Review*, July/August: 32–8.

Woodard, Beth S. (2003) 'Technology and the constructivist learning environment: implications for teaching information literacy skills', *Research Strategies*, 19: 181–92.

Further reading

EDUCAUSE Review, July/August 2005.

Freeman, Geoffrey T. (ed.) (2005) *Library as Place: Rethinking Roles, Rethinking Space*, Vol. 129. Washington, DC: Council on Library and Information Resources; available at: *www.clir.org/pubs/reports/ pub129/pub129.pdf* (accessed: 30 November 2005).

Oblinger, Diana G. and Oblinger, James L. (eds) (2005) *Educating the Net Generation*. EDUCAUSE; available at: *www.educause.edu/educatingthenetgen/* (accessed: 22 February 2006).

Shill, Harold B. and Tonner, Shawn (2003) 'Creating a better place: physical improvements in academic libraries, 1995–2002', *College & Research Libraries*, 64(6): 431–66.

Shill, Harold B. and Tonner, Shawn (2004) 'Does the building still matter? Usage patterns in new, expanded, and renovated libraries, 1995–2002', *College & Research Libraries*, 65(2): 123–50.

6

Libraries in the course management systems learning environment

Jane Quigley, Barbara Knauff and Susan Fliss

It is 11pm. Maya, a student taking a government senior seminar, is working on her final research paper for the term. She is scheduled to present a PowerPoint session on her research findings so far and an annotated bibliography in class the next day. An environmental studies major, she has chosen as a topic the privatisation of hydropower in developing countries. Maya logs into Blackboard, her institution's course management system, and visits the government seminar website to review the comments on one component of her project, a preliminary annotated bibliography. After reading the comments of the professor and the librarian who reviewed her bibliography, she realises that she needs one or two more recently published relevant articles to shore up one aspect of her argument. She locates the guide to recommended resources that the librarian posted in the course site, chooses a suitable article index and goes to work. Having found several useful articles, she incorporates the new material into her presentation... but because it is now so late, she is tired and uncertain about the result. She thinks about e-mailing other students in the class for advice, but because it is a government seminar she feels they may not be able to provide the environmental perspective that she needs. Instead, she uses Blackboard to contact her buddies in an organisation site specifically created for environmental studies majors. She uploads her revised PowerPoint presentation to a workspace in the organisation site and asks for comments on the new material. Meanwhile, Maya sets to work formatting the final bibliography. Remembering a useful guide that was posted by a librarian for a course two semesters back, she finds her way to that course site, which is still available to her, finds the information she needs and finishes the bibliography. An hour later she returns to the environmental studies majors' organisation site and finds that two people have posted positive comments, and one has suggested an easy grammatical improvement. Reassured, Maya uploads her final project to the government seminar website and logs out of Blackboard.

Course management systems

Course management systems (CMSs), often also referred to as virtual learning environments (VLEs), are software systems which facilitate the administration of courses for teachers and learners. Usually accessed and administered through a web browser, these systems allow faculty easy control over course websites. A suite of interactive tools, such as discussion boards, chatrooms, drop boxes for file exchange etc., is generally included to facilitate class work and communication. Common uses of CMSs include distance education courses delivered entirely online in the context of a CMS or in a hybrid or blended solution in which the online CMS supplements the traditional face-to-face course experience. The adoption of CMSs in higher education is reaching the point where they are nearly universally present. A 2005 ECAR study on student use of information technology reported that 72 per cent of students surveyed had used a CMS (Kvavik and Caruso, 2005), and those numbers are increasing.

A number of different CMS products are available, ranging from enterprise-level systems that offer great flexibility and integration with other campus systems to more limited installations. The field is split between commercial products, such as ANGEL, Blackboard, Desire2Learn and WebCT (acquired by Blackboard in 2005), and open-source initiatives such as Moodle and Sakai.

Many CMSs are also integrating related technologies, most notably e-portfolios, which allow students to build a record of and reflection on their educational experience beyond the context of a single class, and content management systems, which allow users to manage and share digital assets, again usually beyond the confines of the single course. Some CMSs even aspire to serving as campus portals, providing personalised and integrated access to a host of services: course sites, content repositories, registrar and financial aid services and other institution-wide systems.

CMSs and student learning

Ideally, both the design of courses within any CMS and the decision to use a given set of features or tools are driven by a focus on the learner. The CMS originated as a tool to enable online classes or to extend the traditional classroom. While this functionality is still central, many of the more recent developments in CMS technology, such as the inclusion of e-portfolios, student weblogs or wikis, are meant to enable student learning beyond the context of a regular 50- or 90-minute class. CMSs are evolving from course-centred content repositories into virtual learning spaces where learners can construct their own knowledge and collaborate with peers. Such developments magnify the CMS's transformative potential for learning: whether in the context of a single class or in the wider context of a user's learning experience, a CMS's great strength is its support for learner-centred pedagogical principles. A CMS can increase communication (between instructor and learner and between learners), increase feedback loops that orient learners towards learning outcomes and greatly facilitate group work. Used well, according to Carmean and Haefner (2002), a CMS can promote 'deeper learning principles' where learning becomes social, active, contextual, engaging and student-owned.

CMS-library integration

Similarly, library strategies aimed at establishing a presence within an institution's CMS are evolving. From simply facilitating access to library resources and services by introducing links to the more challenging task of introducing and assessing information literacy concepts and skills to students within their course and workspace, libraries are adopting a variety of approaches. At one end of the spectrum, library and information-literacy components within a CMS can build upon many of the same dimensions that characterise a highly developed and engaging CMS learning environment – they can be social and interactive, build upon prior knowledge, connect directly to the current learning experience and allow students to control and direct their learning. These principles are increasingly informing librarians' teaching in the classroom as well as in CMS settings – as evidenced by the adoption of active learning methods and awareness of different learning styles and assessment practices.

Many successful library/CMS integration strategies take advantage of CMSs' diverse and highly developed communication tools. A recent ECAR study (Kvavik and Caruso, 2005) of students and information technology reports that students recognise that the use of technology in classrooms heightens their ability to communicate with the instructor and classmates, and enhances opportunities for collaboration and receiving and giving prompt feedback. Librarians can expand their opportunities to communicate with students far beyond the one-hour in-class instruction session that is typical of many courses by participating in discussion threads and offering a chat reference service or a 'virtual office hour' when a librarian will answer questions either by chat or via a discussion thread. CMSs can offer other communication and productivity tools, such as blogs and wikis, which readily lend themselves to use as a research journal or a group bibliography project. Librarians can contribute to group projects, assuming the role of 'information adviser' in each group.

Tools built into the CMS such as quizzes and surveys also allow librarians to engage students with activities related to research and library skills. A librarian who is scheduled to meet with a class can use a quick survey before the session to determine the students' level of experience and skill, and to lay a foundation on which to build during the class session. Post-session surveys allow the librarian to evaluate the effectiveness of the session, invite further questions and follow up with individuals or with the whole class. These activities can clarify and reinforce concepts demonstrated in class through examples and practice exercises, and are helpful for students who may learn better through doing than through hearing or observing.

Resources and scalability

Often the presentation of library resources and services within Blackboard is tailored to the specific needs of students within a particular course. Interactions with students via the CMS-enabled communication channels described above (discussion lists, research journals/blogs, quizzes and surveys) are prime examples of this course-specific integration. Other examples include links to course reserves readings, a page or section highlighting recommended library resources or a fully developed research guide helping students through the process of finding useful information for their research topics. Research guides can range from the very general (e.g. 'getting started with research') to discipline-specific (e.g. 'a research guide to early American history') and topic-specific guides developed for a single class (ENVS 7 – Environmental History). Shank and Dewald (2003) labelled this highly customised approach 'microlevel' integration, as opposed to 'macrolevel' approaches that operate at the broader system level.

Such customised, 'micro' levels of library integration, while ideal in many ways, present several challenges that limit their potential as a universally appropriate solution. One of the most significant is time – it is not practical (or even possible) for librarians to spend the time and effort required to develop such an intense level of support for each CMS class, or perhaps even for very many of them. Additionally, a high level of participation in a course requires a good working relationship and good communication between the faculty member and the librarian, which may take time to establish and may not be realistic in all instances or at all institutions.

Many libraries have adopted a blended approach, mixing micro- and macro-level strategies to allow them to maximise the impact of their efforts. Macro-level strategies – by definition more scalable than the customised micro-level integrations – generally operate at the top level of the CMS rather than within a specific course, and may consist of a simple link to the library, a library tab or page or links to library components such as interlibrary loan, reference help (e-mail or chat reference) or the catalogue or the course reserves system. Some libraries have developed independent tutorials, self-contained information-literacy modules that are available for any student or faculty member to include. In addition, the Texas Information Literacy Tutorial (TILT) can be integrated in CMSs such as Blackboard and WebCT. Some enterprise-level systems allow for building-blocks to be developed, which can facilitate access to bibliographic management software such as RefWorks.

Learning environments

At present many CMS courses are still structured much like traditional classroom environments, with relatively few opportunities for students to construct or contribute to their own learning environments. At least in part, this may be due to faculty struggling to master new technology and trying to adapt the CMS to resemble most closely the teaching model with which they are most familiar. However, as faculty comfort with the technology grows, Richard N. Katz (2003: 56) predicts that there may be a shift towards 'thoughtful experimentation... with new techniques to use the CMS to restructure instruction for more effective results'. Libraries, too, can experiment with new approaches to building information competence among students, moving away from sole reliance on the one-shot, lecture-demo instruction session towards encouraging and facilitating the development of student-built research spaces and customised research modules that give students greater control over their research environment. In a move to give students greater flexibility, Blackboard has developed Blackboard Backpack which allows students to synchronise their personal computers with the CMS, so they have offline access to their course content and can easily organise, annotate and search the materials.

Libraries and IT departments can collaborate to provide a space such as 'My library' or 'My research' where students can add research-related modules independently of their (faculty-controlled) course materials – Van Weigel (2005: 199) calls this a '360° Out-of-the-Course capability'. Enterprise-level CMSs allow a significant amount of customisation by the student, including the option to add or remove content modules to a space within their CMS account. Libraries can develop a variety of modules for the CMS environment – library catalogue 'quick-search' modules, federated database article search modules, 'ask-a-librarian' modules or modules providing quick links to heavily used library services. These have the advantage of scalability, as discussed above, but may not be as course-relevant or contextual as desired. With more effort, libraries can provide discipline-specific modules offering links to a few core reference resources, article databases, subject guides and a contact link for a subject librarian, allowing students the option of populating their CMS space with a few helpful resource modules according to their course-related or research-related interests.

Figure 6.1 Example of a 'My research' module

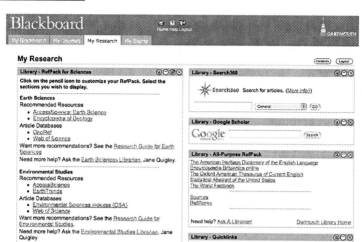

For Dartmouth's Blackboard implementation, a library/IT team created a 'My research' space that students can populate with customisable resource modules (Figure 6.1).

Collaborative culture

CMSs are ubiquitous on campuses and have prompted and encouraged new collaboration between faculty, students, IT and librarians. CMS implementation, development and training provide possibilities for collaboration and strengthening institutional relationships. Librarians and IT staff can jointly present workshops for faculty, organised by academic departments, that address the specific ways a CMS can be used within a discipline for teaching. Both groups can collaborate with faculty to develop a clear information architecture for their online course. All of these constituent groups, including students, can collaboratively design assignments that introduce research skills and concepts to students. Student input is invaluable.

133

Institutions can introduce a CMS to librarians within an environment of support. Give each librarian a test course of his or her own to practise on and develop. An instructional technologist and a librarian can team up to provide workshops to librarians in using CMSs. Even though the CMS may be supported by IT, if librarians approach faculty to integrate library resources into their courses, librarians may find themselves in a position to help faculty members with some technical questions. (CMSs typically allow faculty owners of a course to add instructors, such as librarians and instructional technologists, to the course with different levels of access. For example, a reference librarian might be added as a course builder, allowing him/her to add content and monitor discussions, but not access the online gradebook.) Similarly, librarians and instructional technologists can co-develop and co-teach CMS workshops to faculty and staff. Librarians and other constituents involved in information literacy can co-develop new units or modules to use in courses or library sessions.

At institutions where the CMS is managed by the library, or where the library and IT services are merged or communicate and collaborate well together, interoperability between the CMS and library systems tends to be more robust. Rather than developing systems separately and considering integration as an afterthought, integration is considered front and central. CMS users at such institutions will be more likely to enjoy seamless access from e-reserves to their course websites and vice versa, for example, or central digital asset management which is accessible from both within the CMS and outside. Collaboration can become difficult when it comes to issues of control, even within an organisation. Trust is needed between the group running the CMS and librarians developing CMS modules, because the librarians will need access to the development and production servers.

Collaboration between the library and IT departments is crucial when it comes to systems development, especially as new systems are being brought online. Collaboration and a joint planning effort can ensure that new systems will be able to 'talk to each other', avoid duplication of functionality and minimise custom programming retrofitting to integrate data across systems. If, for example, the library needs a new e-reserves system or a new content management solution, integration with the CMS should be kept in mind at all times. Any such system which is available not only as a stand-alone service but can be accessed from within the CMS as well will probably see more use, and provide a more usable experience to the entire campus community.

Future directions

CMSs are continuously evolving and require continuous efforts to integrate different systems. For example, a professor who wants to make a PowerPoint presentation on recent developments in stem cell research or any other digital learning object available to students should be able to upload this piece of content into a digital content repository via the mechanism of her or his choice, be it the CMS or a separate content management system interface. The teacher should be able to share the content with one or several classes through the CMS, or make it available to any user group of his or her choosing and definition. A student who refines an assignment in the context of the CMS, for example through several feedback iterations with an instructor or peers, should be able to add the polished document seamlessly to his or her e-portfolio from right within the CMS (Figure 6.2).

What will CMSs look like with new technical advancements such as 3D web browsing capability? How

Figure 6.2   An example of a collaborative workspace in the CMS that transcends traditional course boundaries

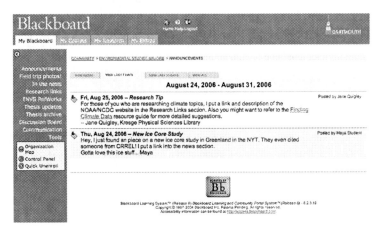

will information discovery tools – such as a federated search system querying of library catalogues, article databases and the web – become integral to the CMS? How will this support our learners and teachers? Rather than serve as a single-purpose application whose mission is to support course websites and mirror the curricular structure of the institution, the CMS of the future will evolve as a fluid application, highly integrated with other digital resources, which will allow individual users to define and structure their own digital learning spaces, giving each user greater control over their own learning outcomes. Educators will continue to develop their understanding of how the CMS contributes to student learning and creates a learner-centred space rather than just an extension of the classroom. The CMS learning environment offers librarians a greater teaching role, and opportunities to contribute to teaching and learning within this CMS learning environment and to collaborate with other constituents within and among institutions of learning.

References

Carmean, Colleen and Haefner, Jeremy (2002) 'Mind over matter: transforming course management systems into effective learning environments', *EDUCAUSE Review*, 37(6): 26–34.

Katz, Richard N. (2003) 'Balancing technology and tradition: the example of course management systems', *EDUCAUSE Review*, 38(4): 48–59.

Kvavik, Robert B. and Caruso, Judith B. (2005) 'The promise and performance of course management systems', in *ECAR Study of Students and Information Technology, 2005: Convenience, Connection, Control, and Learning*, ECAR Research Studies, Vol. 6. Boulder, CO: EDUCAUSE Center for Applied Research, pp. 75–85.

Shank, John D. and Dewald, Nancy H. (2003) 'Establishing our presence in courseware: adding library services to the virtual classroom', *Information Technology and Libraries*, 22(1): 38–43.

Weigel, Van (2005) 'From course management to curricular capabilities: a capabilities approach for the next-generation CMS', in Patricia McGee, Colleen Carmean and Ali Jafari (eds) *Course Management Systems for Learning: Beyond Accidental Pedagogy*. Hershey, PA: Information Science Publishing, pp. 190–205; also published in *EDUCAUSE Review*, 40(3): 54–67.

Further reading

Costello, Barbara, Lenholt, Rob and Stryker, Judson (2004) 'Using Blackboard in library instruction: addressing the learning styles of Generations X and Y', *Journal of Academic Librarianship*, 30(6): 452–60.

Gibbons, Susan (2005) 'Library course-management systems: an overview', *Library Technology Reports*, 41(3): 4–49.

Lippincott, Joan (2005) 'Libraries, information, and course management systems', in Patricia McGee, Colleen Carmean and Ali Jafari (eds) *Course Management Systems for Learning: Beyond Accidental Pedagogy.* Hershey, PA: Information Science Publishing, pp. 39–56.

McGee, Patricia, Carmean, Colleen and Jafari, Ali (eds) (2005) *Course Management Systems For Learning: Beyond Accidental Pedagogy.* Hershey, PA: Information Science Publishing.

Regan, Alison E. and Walcher, Sheldon (2005) 'Environmentalist approaches to portals and course management systems', *Journal of Library Administration*, 43(1/2): 173–88.

Ullman, Craig and Rabinowitz, Mitchell (2004) 'Course management systems and the reinvention of instruction', *THE Journal*, 1 October; available at: *www.thejournal.com/articles/17014* (accessed: 18 October 2006).

7

Academic librarians in the age of videoconferencing: tools for teaching, collaboration and professional development

Susan Fliss, Colleen Wheeler and Calvin Williams

Videoconferencing opens rich new avenues for accessing people, sharing information and constructing knowledge interactively. Today, academic librarians can consult distant colleagues for collaboration; tap experts for perspectives and exchanges in nearly any speciality, including library science, instructional technology, the sciences and the arts and humanities; and access content that may be unavailable locally, including professional development, language immersion and course-sharing. The potential of videoconferencing is especially attractive for those wishing to expand both the reach and the resources of their academic departments and libraries.

Teaching and learning with videoconferencing

Videoconferencing can mitigate barriers of time and distance and enable closer involvement between librarians and colleagues, students and faculty and experts and novices. In higher education videoconferencing is being used in pedagogical applications, professional development and collaborative inter-institutional meetings. Below are several examples of how videoconferencing can be used in support of learning.

In 2005 Wheaton College in Norton, Massachusetts, and the National Institute for Technology in Liberal Education (NITLE) co-sponsored a music composition contest called 'Composers of Internet2' (CI2 – www.wheatoncollege.edu/IT_S/internet2/CI2/). In March 2005 CI2's five students participated in videoconferences during which they enjoyed a performance of their compositions, coaching from a panel of professional composers and insight from a performer's perspective. Connected sites included Wheaton College, the University of Alabama at Birmingham, the University of Pittsburgh and the University of Southern Florida. All five students took advantage of an offer to revise their work based on session feedback. Their final compositions were premiered in a public concert, which was webcast live, at Hulsey Recital Hall at the University of Alabama at Birmingham in June 2005. Finally, each young composer received a professional recording and a monetary award.

In addition to receiving guidance from professors from Wheaton College, the University of Alabama at Birmingham, Birmingham Southern College and the University of Pittsburgh, participants benefited from interactions with members of their community of practice, exposure to related careers and access to a broad listening audience.

The best part of the experience for one of the CI2 students was 'hearing feedback from completely new sources. In working with just one composer, you only really hear one opinion; it was nice to hear different opinions, especially from people who had never met me and never seen any of my other work.' Many commented that they found the performer's perspective eye-opening, particularly in terms of technique. One of the CI2 coaches reported, 'The greatest part for me was coaching a student from a great distance with the benefit of a live reading. The latter is a crucial element in a young composer's development.'

Faculty teaching foreign languages turn to videoconferencing to simulate an immersion experience for students on campus. In 2004 Wheaton College students in Jonathan Walsh's class, 'Introduction to French Culture', studied Franco-American relations. Walsh arranged for his American students to meet with French counterparts attending ITIN (l'école supérieure d'informatique), a technical university outside Paris, for one videoconferencing session. The purpose of the exchange was to debate Franco-American issues, including Franco-American relations since the Iraq war and Francophobia or 'French-bashing'.

Before the videoconferencing session Walsh was concerned about how students on both sides of the Atlantic would interact and moderate potentially 'tricky political territory'. The French students were mainly male programmers with some liberal arts studies experience and spoke English fairly well; the Wheaton students' French language ability was advanced intermediate. Before the first exchange students spent two weeks studying assigned readings and preparing answers to questions. Walsh stresses the importance of good preparation and believes that 'assigning a common reading was a key component to the success of the students' interactions'.

Walsh opted to introduce a controversial topic to help spark conversation. Students were respectful of each other during the sessions and the controversial topic got them thinking beyond language and technology. During the exchange the French students were very sympathetic and gracious about the American students' language ability. Walsh believes this was the best outcome for the type of preparation they did.

The goal was to have the students really communicate and, at times, the students got off topic and asked personal questions. The French took this opportunity to engage the Americans about their views on the Iraq war and the obesity issue in the USA. Walsh thinks the conversation dispelled some stereotypes. 'The French were impressed by our students. Through videoconferencing they became real people and their personalities came out. I believe that personalities emerged in part because the videoconferencing quality was so good it was like being in the same room.'

Walsh advocates testing connections before the class and, while he did not bring the students in for practice beforehand, he believes it would be beneficial for participants to become familiar with the technology before the interaction.

Videoconferencing is a powerful technology for approximating an immersion experience for language and culture. Students study at Wheaton for two to three years before travelling abroad. Videoconferencing offers them an international experience sooner in their educational career and before they travel. In a future class Walsh would like to identify a topic that would interest students in francophone Africa, envisioning a three-way dialogue between Norton, Massachusetts, and possible locations including Paris, Mali and Quebec.

Another language immersion experience is to connect students to experts or notable individuals from other cultures. In February 2006 Dartmouth College students in Annabel Martin's Spanish senior seminar, 'The Lead Generation: Basque Terrorism and the Nation', studied the works of several Basque writers and artists. They also had the opportunity to meet the artists to discuss democracy and the arts in the Basque country. From Spain through videoconferencing, Basque film-maker Helena Taberna, novelist Bernardo Atxaga, poet Julia Otxoa and sculptor Ricardo Ugarte joined the class to discuss their works.

Martin shared her impression of the experience:

> It was fabulous. It made me feel like I had travelled to Spain and back in the course of the two hours. I think this is a fantastic way to enhance student learning. The cameras allow for a good hook-up between the two sites... and you really do feel like you're having a conversation with the people on the other end. The students loved it. You can't imagine how star-struck they were to see the artists there in person. They prepared very well for the experience and felt very privileged to have this opportunity.

While pedagogical uses for videoconferencing are apparent for foreign language courses, this technology is being used in the sciences as well. Through the Office of Marine Programs at the University of Rhode Island, middle-school students from 20 of the state's K-12 schools virtually explored the hard-to-reach *Titanic* 'live'. 'Using state-of-the-art imagery and equipment, they inspected the ship to see how it has withstood both natural changes and human exploration over the past two decades' (www.ri.net/RINET/ products/ivid/projectgallery.html).

In another Rhode Island project a middle-school teacher joined Earthwatch researchers in Florida, becoming a kind of 'embedded' researcher. She participated in gathering data about manatees, monitored the research team's progress and communicated daily with her students back in her classroom, sharing her experiences through photographs, journal entries, webpages and several videoconferences. Her students contributed to the work of the research team by participating in data gathering and analysis. The programme was funded by the Earthwatch Institute with a grant from the Rhode Island Foundation.

In the realm of the arts and humanities, artists and students are gathering virtually via videoconferencing. Ann Doyle, Internet2's manager for arts and humanities initiatives, has produced many notable collaborations in the performing arts. 'Virtual Halloween at the Rialto' (Georgia State University) and 'Cultivating Communities: Dance in the Digital Age' (University of Southern California) involve advanced technology running over Internet2.

Using more common videoconferencing tools, the 'Slide Heard Round the World' (www.wheatoncollege.edu/it_s/internet2/trombone/) connects trombone players in a kind of virtual community. This annual series of events features master classes, performances, lectures and discussion on topics of interest to trombonists of all ages and abilities. Student and professional musicians, instrument designers, editors and composers 'meet' through Internet2-connected sites. Events are available for public viewing and comment as live and archived streams over the commodity internet.

Professional development

Through periodic meetings via videoconferencing, librarians, information technologists, curricular designers, faculty and students from different institutions can identify ways to collaborate to support teaching, learning and research in their academic communities. Every campus grapples with the same questions. Where do our institutions want to be in providing high-quality library and IT services? What are the shared needs on our respective campuses? How can our constituent groups partner to meet these teaching, learning and research needs? Opening a dialogue with other campuses around these questions can help participants articulate issues and identify solutions, and may spark inter-institutional collaboration.

Wheaton College, Monmouth University and Dartmouth College brought librarians and instructional technologists together via videoconferencing to explore and share experiences with library/IT collaboration. Session participants identified techniques and tools to discover, develop and implement new collaborative initiatives with the ultimate goal of achieving maximum integration of information-literacy and technology skills into the teaching and learning process in their institutions.

Four sessions allowed participants to meet one another and gain experience with videoconferencing technology. Participants reported that:

- the barriers to speaking were not as high as they had expected;
- pseudo-face-to-face meetings are an efficient way to meet without travelling;
- the sessions about what other institutions are doing led to valuable local conversations and collaborations.

Suggestions for improving this communication experience included:

- getting to know one another better and earlier would have enhanced the conversations;
- have an initial face-to-face meeting for all participants at a mutually convenient location;

- create a participant reference roster that includes names, institutions, roles, thumbnail photos and contact information;
- schedule a 30-minute local meeting before each session;
- use identification protocols during the sessions (stating name before speaking, showing names on screen).

These sessions brought librarians and instructional technologists together from three different institutions to share experiences and investigate issues. The conversations revealed the different points of view among the participants, the different campus cultures and the similarities in the goals to support the teaching and learning on campuses.

Professional conferences

Professional conferences are incorporating videoconferencing technology to host guest speakers, connect audiences located in different parts of the country or the world and even to host conferences entirely online.

At a day-long North East Regional Computing Program (NERCOMP – www.nercomp.org/) conference on 19 January 2005 on 'Hiring, Training and Managing Student Workers', Lynn Stipick, director of the Student Technology Assistant Program at Monmouth University, prepared to give her presentation at 11am. Stipick's topic was using a learning management system (LMS) to manage student technology assistants. Co-worker Wendy Savoth and two student employees joined Stipick on the panel; however, only Stipick had travelled to Massachusetts – Savoth and the students participated from Monmouth's campus in New Jersey via Skype, a voice-over-IP desktop videoconferencing system.

The panellists shared their experiences of applying an LMS for student workers with the audience; at the same time they demonstrated the use of desktop videoconferencing technology.

Thinking about her role as a long-distance participant in the session, Savoth reflected: 'The potential of using this technology in teaching and learning opens many avenues of possibilities. It also seems to be another testimony to how technology is bringing the world closer and closer together.' Stipick was encouraged by this technology and would present using videoconferencing again. She sees applications for Skype-like products in her own work and plans to use it to communicate with students working in the various labs on campus who are troubleshooting computer problems. Faculty and staff in university departments can use this technology to communicate among themselves and with students when they are out of town... or even across campus.

Professional organisations with different focuses can bring their constituents together to discuss mutual topics of interest via videoconferencing. For the first time, in April 2006 the library and IT organisations of the Association of College and Research Libraries (ACRL), EDUCAUSE and the Coalition for Networked Information (CNI) sponsored a joint virtual conference: 'Innovate and Motivate: Next Generation Libraries'. The goal of the conference was 'to explore how revolutions in technology impact academic librarianship and higher education'. The virtual conference included keynote speakers, asynchronous poster sessions and synchronous roundtable discussions. These organisations brought different constituent groups together to discuss, learn, debate and frame a vision for the future of libraries.

Videoconferencing technology

If you are familiar with Moore's Law (Gordon Moore's 1965 prediction of technological developments that would double the number of transistors on a chip every two years), then you are aware of the forces that have driven rapid advances in videoconferencing. AT&T, at the 1964 New York World's Fair, announced a breakthrough in the telecommunications industry, the inauguration of the Picturephone, setting in motion an unprecedented growth in the development of information and communication technologies. Yesterday's Picturephone has evolved into a web-based conferencing resource.

Web-based conferencing resources include tools built on top of two technologies: 'video over IP' and 'voice over IP' (VoIP). Video over IP uses newer technology that allows video signals to be streamed and managed over the internet. Digital video compression standards have made it possible for audio and video signals to be transmitted seamlessly over a digital network. There are three commonly used categories of video presentations: videoconferencing, video broadcasting and video on demand (www.siemon.com/sg/white_papers/03-08-26-VideoOverIP.asp).

Of these three presentation types, videoconferencing is the only one that allows a person to transmit video data in two directions simultaneously (full-duplex), as opposed to a connection where only one person can transmit at a time (half-duplex). As an example, think of a telephone conversation where both parties can talk and be heard at the same time. A video camera at both ends of a connection accommodates this kind of give-and-take, allowing users to interact more naturally and accommodating capture and transmission of video and audio signals at the same time.

Video broadcasting is different; its one-way video transmission is more akin to an open pipe where the receiver must await a signal from the sender. Academic librarians will see this type of transmission being used to deliver presentations, training events and lectures. Video broadcast is done in two modes: unicast or multicast. Unicast transfer mode is considered by many to be the leading alternative for transmitting information on a data network. Any time you get or send data using HTTP, SMTP or FTP, you are sending and receiving one-way (unicast) information. Multicast transfer mode enables the sender to distribute data to multiple locations from a single starting point; consider a television station sending out a video signal from one server to many receivers.

Video on demand, also called VOD, allows a user to select and watch video-recorded content while data are being streamed over a network. Video on demand is primarily used in entertainment and videoconferencing.

VoIP combines the best of data and voice networking technologies, making possible real-time conversations over the internet (www.lightreading.com/document.asp?doc_id=40811). Users should be aware that VoIP is not a secure telephone service, requires a broadband connection and can be disabled by power outages and slow broadband connections. VoIP allows the transmission of an analogue voice signal over a networked environment; it gives the user options for sending and receiving data using familiar devices such as a desktop telephone, wireless devices such as cell phones or computers connected to the internet. It is worth noting that the authors of this chapter used a VoIP tool called Skype in conjunction with a web-based editing tool called Writely to collaborate on creating this chapter.

Future developments

Videoconferencing can be combined with other technology-mediated tools to build rich hybrid learning experiences. Pam Christman, director of Technology Programs and Network Services at the Rhode Island Network for Educational Technology (RINET), has developed a tremendous collection of projects using this collaborative approach:

> Consider videoconferencing and video streaming as emerging types of interactive, collaborative content. For instance, one librarian might connect a student and a collaborator (or subject expert) together in a videoconference where the parties work together to combine and create new content by accessing a shared electron microscope. Another librarian might connect a student with a museum video stream where the student virtually walks around a sculpture and gains new perspectives that could not be realised via a two-dimensional representation of the artwork. In these ways, librarians assist students in creating new content and using new perspectives available to them from content partners rather than content creators such as academic institutions, museums, zoos, aquariums, businesses, etc.

Today a new brand of professional conference is evolving – one that offers access to relevant pre- and post-conference content and an array of options for interaction with other conference attendees. Emerging options include tools for creating knowledge with others (such as wikis) and personal broadcasting (such as podcasts and blogs). Collaborating groups will be able to combine tools to create useful working and learning environments as needed. Imagine a cross-disciplinary team that co-develops an online gaming and simulation environment to provide students with an engaging way to learn and use information-literacy and technology fluency skills. The development team of librarians, instructional designers, faculty and students could elect to use videoconferencing to conduct regular full-team check-ins, consult with gaming design experts and carry out user testing with local focus groups. Individual members of the team could use VoIP for one-to-one work sessions. They may contribute their end product and the information gathered from their work to an open repository for peer review and improvement, such as the LoLa Exchange (www.lolaexchange.org/). The game may be used in several institutions' learning commons and accessed from the libraries' websites.

In addition to taking advantage of these tools for their own learning, academic librarians can use them to connect with students needing help at critical navigation points in their research. Virtual reference with videoconferencing capabilities creates a more personal and less mechanical environment in which to engage students. The potential exists to connect with library users conducting research in remote locations or on study abroad, or even in a dorm or coffeeshop across campus. Librarians can create a comfortable, effective and efficient consulting environment for users with internet access anywhere.

People interested in using videoconferencing need to be aware of the implications of the US Telecommunications Act 1996, which is being rewritten as this chapter goes to print. The internet has become a powerful commercial tool – and a political one. The last ten years have seen a consolidation of the telecommunications industry and an opportunity for traditional telephone companies to lobby for becoming all-powerful providers of voice, video and data. George Loftus, executive director of the Ocean State Higher Education Economic Development and Administrative Network (OSHEAN), urges academic librarians to 'pay attention and engage in the policy groups within your professional organizations'. Issues like 'network neutrality' and CALEA (Communications Assistance for Law Enforcement Act) are being hotly debated now; they may have sobering implications for free and equitable access to information.

Conclusion

Videoconferencing is becoming commonplace in higher education and presents innovative opportunities for librarians to integrate this mode of communication in their teaching, professional development, research into information issues and participation in the teaching and research missions of educational institutions. This chapter presents several examples of creative applications of videoconferencing. In seeking to apply them to academic librarianship, librarians may need to expand their role within and outside their library to be successful, connecting disparate areas within the organisation and coaching colleagues in doing the same. What does it mean for academic librarians if 'anyone can collaborate with anyone else, anytime, anywhere'? Where are the opportunities for academic librarians? What are the benefits? Just imagine...

Note

Readers are invited to share their videoconferencing experiences via the CDA site: www.wheatoncollege.edu/it_s/internet2/CDA/.

Conclusion
Joe M. Williams

As mentioned in the Introduction, we hope this handbook provides a quick and useful overview of some of today's most current technologies, and that it helps you choose those technologies that will enhance and define your changing instructional services. As the examples, discussions and case studies in the preceding chapters illustrate, there are a great many technologies available today to extend and enhance library instructional services.

The future of many of the technologies discussed here, the chapter authors suggest, will generally provide increased interactivity and personalisation options to the user, and continuing improvements in computing and networking speed and storage capabilities. For example, highly interactive and immersive gaming mechanics may become a very common and expected type of interactivity in web-based tutorials and other forms of online library instruction. Virtual reference and instruction services may begin to incorporate more personalisation features, such as on-screen annotation and improved co-browsing functionality. Library instructional vidcast and podcast offerings may become more prevalent, giving patrons more flexibility and control in getting their specific instructional needs fulfilled. Continued improvements in personal computing hardware and networking infrastructure will also contribute to growth in this area, as well as in mobile computing and flexible, personalised learning spaces. Course management systems will continue to synthesise all of these developing technologies into virtual learning spaces, with the addition of synchronous videoconferencing to connect students and instructors at a distance.

Technologies will continue to mature and change over time, which will continue to affect library patron needs and expectations. As noted throughout this book, instruction and technology both play integral roles in librarianship today. This handbook aims to bring these two relevant topics together in a practical overview of instructional uses and applications of today's popular technologies. Hopefully, it will serve as a useful tool as you test and choose specific technologies to enhance and define your library's changing instructional services.

Index

Printed in the United Kingdom
by Lightning Source UK Ltd.
127230UK00002B/235-240/A